Blockchain

for
dummies®
A Wiley Brand

Blockchain

by Tiana Laurence

Blockchain For Dummies®

Published by: **John Wiley & Sons, Inc.**, 111 River Street, Hoboken, NJ 07030-5774, www.wiley.com

Copyright © 2017 by John Wiley & Sons, Inc., Hoboken, New Jersey

Published simultaneously in Canada

For general information on our other products and services, please contact our Customer Care Department within the U.S. at 877-762-2974, outside the U.S. at 317-572-3993, or fax 317-572-4002. For technical support, please visit https://hub.wiley.com/community/support/dummies.

Wiley publishes in a variety of print and electronic formats and by print-on-demand. Some material included with standard print versions of this book may not be included in e-books or in print-on-demand. If this book refers to media such as a CD or DVD that is not included in the version you purchased, you may download this material at http://booksupport.wiley.com. For more information about Wiley products, visit www.wiley.com.

Library of Congress Control Number: 2017936813

ISBN 978-1-119-36559-4 (pbk); ISBN 978-1-119-36561-7 (ebk); ISBN 978-1-119-36560-0 (ebk)

Manufactured in the United States of America

10 9 8 7 6 5 4 3 2 1

Contents at a Glance

Table of Contents

Introduction

Welcome to *Blockchain For Dummies!* If you want to find out what blockchains are and the basics of how to use them, this is the book for you. Many people think blockchains are difficult to understand. They might also think that blockchains are just about cryptocurrencies like Bitcoin, but they're are so much more. Anyone can master the basics of blockchains.

In this book, you find helpful advice for navigating the blockchain world and cryptocurrencies that run them. You also find practical step-by-step tutorials that will build your understanding of how blockchains work and where they add value. You don't need a background in programming, economics, or world affairs to understand this book, but I do touch on all these subjects because blockchain technology intersects all of them.

About This Book

This book explains the basics of blockchains, smart contracts, and cryptocurrencies. You probably picked up this book because you've heard about blockchains, know they're important, but have no idea what they are, how they work, or why you should care. This book answers all these questions in easy-to-understand terms.

This book is a bit different than just about any other blockchain book on the market. It provides a survey of all the key blockchains in the public market, how they work, what they do, and something useful you can try with them today.

This book also covers the landscape of blockchain technology and points out some of the key things to be aware of for your own blockchain projects. Here, you find out how to install an Ethereum wallet, create and execute a smart contract, make entries into Bitcoin and Factom, and earn cryptocurrencies.

You don't have to read the book cover to cover. Just flip to the subject that you're interested in.

Finally, within this book, you may note that some web addresses break across two lines of text. If you're reading this book in print and want to visit one of these web pages, simply key in the web address exactly as it's noted in the text, pretending as though the line break doesn't exist. If you're reading this as an e-book, you've got it easy — just click the web address to be taken directly to the web page.

Foolish Assumptions

I don't make many assumptions about you and your experience with cryptocurrency, programing, and legal matters but I do assume the following:

» You have a computer and access to the Internet.

» You know the basics of how to use your computer and the Internet.

» You know how to navigate through menus within programs.

» You're new to blockchain and you aren't a skilled programmer. Of course, if you are a skilled programmer, you can still get a lot out of this book — you just may be able to breeze past some of the step-by-step guidelines.

Icons Used in This Book

Throughout this book, I use icons in the margin to draw your attention to certain kinds of information. Here's what the icons mean:

TIP

The Tip icon marks tips and shortcuts that you can use to make blockchains easier to use.

REMEMBER

The Remember icon marks the information that's especially important to know — the stuff you'll want to commit to memory. To siphon off the most important information in each chapter, just skim through these icons.

TECHNICAL STUFF

The Technical Stuff icon marks information of a highly technical nature that you can skip over without missing the main point of the subject at hand.

WARNING

The Warning icon tells you to watch out! It marks important information that may save you headaches — or tokens.

Beyond the Book

In addition to the material in the print or e-book you're reading right now, this product also comes with some access-anywhere goodies on the web. Check out the free Cheat Sheet for more on blockchains. To get this Cheat Sheet, simply go to www.dummies.com and type **Blockchain For Dummies Cheat Sheet** in the Search box.

Where to Go from Here

You can apply blockchain technology to virtually every business domain. Right now there is explosive growth in financial, healthcare, government, insurance industries, and this is just the beginning. The whole world is changing and the possibilities are endless.

1
Getting Started with Blockchain

Discover what blockchains are all about and how they can benefit your organization.

Identify the right type of technology and the four steps to developing and executing an effective blockchain project.

Make your own smart contracts on Bitcoin, and determine where this technology can fit within your organization.

Discover the tools you need to step up and run your own private blockchain on Ethereum.

» **Understanding why they matter**

» **Identifying the three types of blockchains**

» **Deepening your knowledge of how blockchains work**

Chapter **1**

Introducing Blockchain

Originally, *blockchain* was just the computer science term for how to structure and share data. Today blockchains are hailed the "fifth evolution" of computing.

Blockchains are a novel approach to the distributed database. The innovation comes from incorporating old technology in new ways. You can think of blockchains as distributed databases that a group of individuals controls and that store and share information.

There are many different types of blockchains and blockchain applications. Blockchain is an all-encompassing technology that is integrating across platforms and hardware all over the world.

Beginning at the Beginning: What Blockchains Are

A blockchain is a data structure that makes it possible to create a digital ledger of data and share it among a network of independent parties. There are many different types of blockchains.

- » **Public blockchains:** Public blockchains, such as Bitcoin, are large distributed networks that are run through a native token. They're open for anyone to participate at any level and have open-source code that their community maintains.

- » **Permissioned blockchains:** Permissioned blockchains, such as Ripple, control roles that individuals can play within the network. They're still large and distributed systems that use a native token. Their core code may or may not be open source.

- » **Private blockchains:** Private blockchains tend to be smaller and do not utilize a token. Their membership is closely controlled. These types of blockchains are favored by consortiums that have trusted members and trade confidential information.

All three types of blockchains use cryptography to allow each participant on any given network to manage the ledger in a secure way without the need for a central authority to enforce the rules. The removal of central authority from database structure is one of the most important and powerful aspects of blockchains.

REMEMBER

Blockchains create permanent records and histories of transactions, but nothing is really permanent. The permanence of the record is based on the permanence of the network. In the context of blockchains, this means that a large portion of a blockchain community would all have to agree to change the information and are incentivized *not* to change the data.

When data is recorded in a blockchain, it's extremely difficult to change or remove it. When someone wants to add a record to a blockchain, also called a *transaction* or an *entry*, users in the network who have validation control verify the proposed transaction. This is where things get tricky because every blockchain has a slightly different spin on how this should work and who can validate a transaction.

What blockchains do

A blockchain is a peer-to-peer system with no central authority managing data flow. One of the key ways to removing central control while maintaining data integrity is to have a large distributed network of independent users. This means that the computers that make up the network are in more than one location. These computers are often referred to as *full nodes*.

Figure 1-1 shows a visualization of the structure of the Bitcoin blockchain network. You can see it in action at http://dailyblockchain.github.io.

Addred/Transaction details (hover over nodes)

About: Visualization of bitcoin transactions (unconfirmed ones).

Node size scale: LINEAR ○ LOG ◉
LEGEND: Green = input, Red = output, Yellow = input+output, Blue = transaction
NAVIGATION: mouse + scroll = pan/zoom, SPACE = run/pause
TODO:
    - auto remove transactions older then x min or verified
    - show transaction details on hover
    - connect disconnect button
    - listen for a specyfic address and color it and display alert when present

FIGURE 1-1:
The structure of
the Bitcoin
blockchain
network.

To prevent the network from being corrupted, not only are blockchains decentralized but they often also utilize a cryptocurrency. A *cryptocurrency* is a digital token that has a market value. Cryptocurrencies are traded on exchanges like stocks.

Cryptocurrencies work a little differently for each blockchain. Basically, the software pays the hardware to operate. The software is the blockchain protocol. Well-known blockchain protocols include Bitcoin, Ethereum, Ripple, Hyperledger, and Factom. The hardware consists of the full nodes that are securing the data in the network.

Why blockchains matter

Blockchains are now recognized as the "fifth evolution" of computing, the missing trust layer for the Internet. This is one of the reasons that so many people have become excited about this topic.

Blockchains can create trust in digital data. When information has been written into a blockchain database, it's nearly impossible to remove or change it. This capability has never existed before.

When data is permanent and reliable in a digital format, you can transact business online in ways that, in the past, were only possible offline. Everything that has stayed analog, including property rights and identity, can now be created and maintained online. Slow business and banking processes, such as money wires and fund settlements, can now be done nearly instantaneously. The implications for secure digital records are enormous for the global economy.

The first applications created were designed to piggyback on the secure digital value transfer that blockchains enable through the trading of their native tokens. These included things like the movement of money and assets. But the possibilities of the blockchain networks go far beyond the movement of value.

The Structure of Blockchains

Blockchains are composed of three core parts:

>> **Block:** A list of transactions recorded into a ledger over a given period. The size, period, and triggering event for blocks is different for every blockchain.

Not all blockchains are recording and securing a record of the movement of their cryptocurrency as their primary objective. But all blockchain do record the movement of their cryptocurrency or token. Think of the *transaction* as simply being the recording of data. Assigning a value to it (such as happens in a financial transaction) is used to interpret what that data means.

>> **Chain:** A hash that links one block to another, mathematically "chaining" them together. This is one of the most difficult concepts in blockchain to comprehend. It's also the magic that glues blockchains together and allows them to create mathematical trust.

The hash in blockchain is created from the data that was in the previous block. The hash is a fingerprint of this data and locks blocks in order and time.

TECHNICAL STUFF

Although blockchains are a relatively new innovation, hashing is not. Hashing was invented over 30 years ago. This old innovation is being used because it creates a one-way function that cannot be decrypted. A hashing function creates a mathematical algorithm that maps data of any size to a bit string of a fixed size. A bit string is usually 32 characters long, which then represents the data that was hashed. The Secure Hash Algorithm (SHA) is one of some cryptographic hash functions used in blockchains. SHA-256 is a common algorithm that generates an almost-unique, fixed-size 256-bit (32-byte) hash. For practical purposes, think of a hash as a digital fingerprint of data that is used to lock it in place within the blockchain.

>> **Network:** The network is composed of "full nodes." Think of them as the computer running an algorithm that is securing the network. Each node contains a complete record of all the transactions that were ever recorded in that blockchain.

The nodes are located all over the world and can be operated by anyone. It's difficult, expensive, and time-consuming to operate a full node, so people don't do it for free. They're incentivized to operate a node because they want to earn cryptocurrency. The underlying blockchain algorithm rewards them for their service. The reward is usually a token or cryptocurrency, like Bitcoin.

TIP

The terms *Bitcoin* and *blockchain* are often used interchangeably, but they're not the same. Bitcoin has a blockchain. The Bitcoin blockchain is the underlying protocol that enables the secure transfer of Bitcoin. The term *Bitcoin* is the name of the cryptocurrency that powers the Bitcoin network. The blockchain is a class of software, and Bitcoin is a specific cryptocurrency.

Blockchain Applications

Blockchain applications are built around the idea that network is the arbitrator. This type of system is an unforgiving and blind environment. Computer code becomes law, and rules are executed as they were written and interpreted by the network. Computers don't have the same social biases and behaviors as humans do.

The network can't interpret intent (at least not yet). Insurance contracts arbitrated on a blockchain have been heavily investigated as a use case built around this idea.

Another interesting thing that blockchains enable is impeccable record keeping. They can be used to create a clear timeline of who did what and when. Many industries and regulatory bodies spend countless hours trying to asses this problem. Blockchain-enabled record keeping will relieve some of the burdens that are created when we try to interpret the past.

The Blockchain Life Cycle

Blockchains originated with the creation of Bitcoin. It demonstrated that a group of individuals who had never met could operate online within a system that was desensitized to cheat others that were cooperating on the network.

The original Bitcoin network was built to secure the Bitcoin cryptocurrency. It has around 5,000 full nodes and is globally distributed. It's primarily used to trade Bitcoin and exchange value, but the community saw the potential of doing a lot more with the network. Because of its size and time-tested security, it's also being used to secure other smaller blockchains and blockchain applications.

The Ethereum network is a second evolution of the blockchain concept. It takes the traditional blockchain structure and adds a programming language that is built inside of it. Like Bitcoin, it has over 5,000 full nodes and is globally distributed. Ethereum is primarily used to trade Ether, make smart contracts, and create decentralized autonomous organizations (DAOs). It's also being used to secure blockchain applications and smaller blockchains.

The Factom network is the third evolution in blockchain technology. It utilizes a lighter consensus system, incorporates voting, and stores a lot more information. It was built primarily to secure data and system. Factom operates with federated nodes and an unlimited number of auditing nodes. Its network is small, so it anchors itself into other distributed networks building bridges across the carries blockchains.

Consensus: The Driving Force of Blockchains

Blockchains are powerful tools because they create honest systems that self-correct without the need of a third party to enforce the rules. They accomplish the enforcement of rules through their consensus algorithm.

In the blockchain world, *consensus* is the process of developing an agreement among a group of commonly mistrusting shareholders. These are the full nodes on the network. The full nodes are validating transactions that are entered into the network to be recorded as part of the ledger.

Figure 1-2 shows the concept of how blockchains come to agreement.

Each blockchain has its own algorithms for creating agreement within its network on the entries being added. There are many different models for creating consensus because each blockchain is creating different kinds of entries. Some blockchains are trading value, others are storing data, and others are securing systems and contracts.

FIGURE 1-2:
How blockchains
work.

Bitcoin, for example, is trading the value of its token between members on its network. The tokens have a market value, so the requirements related to performance, scalability, consistency, threat model, and failure model will be higher. Bitcoin operates under the assumption that a malicious attacker may want to corrupt the history of trades in order to steal tokens. Bitcoin prevents this from happening by using a consensus model called "proof of work" that solves the Byzantine general's problem: "How do you know that the information you are looking at has not been changed internally or externally?" Because changing or manipulating data is almost always possible, the reliability of data is a big problem for computer science.

Most blockchains operate under the premise that they will be attacked by outside forces or by users of the system. The expected threat and the degree of trust that the network has in the nodes that operate the blockchain will determine the type of consensus algorithm that they use to settle their ledger. For example, Bitcoin and Ethereum expect a very high degree of threat and use a strong consensus algorithm called *proof of work.* There is no trust in the network.

On the other end of the spectrum, blockchains that are used to record financial transactions between known parties can use a lighter and faster consensus. Their need for high-speed transactions is more important. Proof of work is too slow and costly for them to operate because of the comparatively few participants within the network and immediate finality need for each transaction.

Blockchains in Use

Hundreds of blockchains and blockchain applications are in existence today. The whole world has become obsessed with the ideas of moving money faster, incorporating and governing in a distributed network, and building secure applications and hardware.

You can see many of these public blockchains by going to a cryptocurrency exchange.

Figure 1-3 shows the altcoin exchange for Poloniex (https://poloniex.com), a cryptocurrency trading platform.

FIGURE 1-3:
The altcoin exchange platform.

Blockchains are moving beyond the trading value market and are being incorporated into all sorts of industries. Blockchains add a new trust layer that now makes working online secure in a way that was not possible beforehand.

Current blockchain uses

Most up-and-running blockchain applications revolve around moving money or other forms of value quickly and cheaply. This includes trading public company stock, paying employees in other countries, and exchanging one currency for another.

Blockchains are also now being used as part of a software security stack. The U.S. Department of Homeland Security has been investigating blockchain software that secures Internet of Things (IoT) devices. The IoT world has some of the most to gain from this innovation, because it's especially vulnerable to spoofing and other forms of hacking. IoT devices have also become more pervasive, and security has become more reliant on them. Hospital systems, self-driving cars, and safety systems are prime examples.

DAOs are another interesting blockchain innovation. This type of blockchain application represents a new way to organize and incorporate companies online. DAOs have been used to organize and invest funds via the Ethereum network.

Future blockchain applications

Larger and longer-run blockchain projects that are being explored now include government-backed land record systems, identity, and international travel security applications.

The possibilities of a blockchain-infused future have excited the imaginations of business people, governments, political groups, and humanitarians across the world. Countries such as the UK, Singapore, and the United Arab Emirates see it as a way to cut cost, create new financial instruments, and keep clean records. They have active investments and initiatives exploring blockchain.

Blockchains have laid a foundation where the need for trust has been taken out of the equation. Where before asking for "trust" was a big deal, with blockchains it's small. Also, the infrastructure that enforces the rule if that trust is broken can be lighter. Much of society is built on trust and enforcement of rules. The social and economic implications of blockchain applications can be emotionally and politically polarizing because blockchain will change how we structure value-based and socially based transactions.

Chapter 2

Picking a Blockchain

The blockchain industry is complex and growing in size and capabilities every day. When you understand the three core types of blockchains and their limitations, you'll know what's possible with this new technology.

This chapter is all about assessing blockchain technology and developing a project plan. It puts the following chapters about individual blockchain platforms and applications into context.

Here, you see how to assess the three different types of blockchain platforms, what's being built on each type, and why. I give you a few tools that help you outline your project, predict obstacles, and overcome challenges.

Where Blockchains Add Substance

There's a lot of buzz surrounding blockchains and the cryptocurrencies that run them. Some of this buzz just stems from the fluctuation in the value of cryptocurrencies and the fear that blockchain technology will disrupt many industry and government functions. A lot of money has poured into research and development because stakeholders don't want to be made obsolete and entrepreneurs want to explore new business models.

When it comes to finding an opportunity for blockchain technology to add value to an organization, often the question arises, "Where do blockchains add value and how are they different from existing technologies?"

Blockchains are a special type of database. They can be utilized anywhere you would use a normal database — but it may not make sense to go through the trouble and expense of using a blockchain when a normal database can do the job.

You really see value in using some form of a blockchain when you want to share information with parties you don't fully truest, your data needs to be audited, or your data is at risk of being compromised internally or externally. None of these questions are simple, and the correct solutions can be difficult to ascertain.

This section helps narrow down your options.

Determining your needs

Blockchains come in a lot of flavors. You'll find one that matches your needs — the trick is finding it! Mapping your needs to the best blockchain can be overwhelming. Whenever I have lots of options and often conflicting needs, I like to utilize a weighted decision matrix.

A weighted decision matrix is an excellent tool for evaluating the needs of a project and then mapping those needs to possible solutions. The key advantage of the matrix is to help you quantify and prioritize individual needs for your project and simplify decision making. Weighted decision matrixes also prevent you from becoming overwhelmed by individual criteria. If done properly, this tool allows you to converge on single idea that is compatible with all your goals.

To create a weighted decision matrix, follow these steps:

TIP

1. **Brainstorm the key criteria or goals that your team needs to meet.**

   If you aren't sure of the criteria you need to consider when evaluating your blockchain project, here are a few things to keep in mind:

   - Scale and volume
   - Speed and latency
   - Security and immutability
   - Storage capacity and structural needs

   Your team will have its own list of objects and priorities. These are just a few to consider while evaluating the correct platform to use to meet your needs.

2. **Reduce the list of criteria to no more than ten items.**

TIP

   If you're having a hard time refining your list of needs, consider using a comparison matrix tool.

3. **Create a table in Microsoft Excel or a similar program.**

4. **Enter the design criteria in the first column.**

5. **Assign a relative weight to each criterion based on how important that objective is to the success of the project.**

   Limit the number of points to 10 and distribute them between all your criteria — for example, 1 = low, 2 = medium, and 3 = high priority.

TIP

   If you're working in a team, have each member weight the criteria separately.

6. **Add up the numbers for each objective and divide by the number of team members for a composite team weight.**

7. **Make any needed adjustment to weights to make sure each criteria are weighted correctly.**

Congratulations! You now have a ranked list of criteria you need to meet to be successful with your blockchain project.

Defining your goal

You can easily get lost building a blockchain project that doesn't have a clear goal or purpose. Take the time to understand where you and your team would like to go and what the final objective is. For example, a goal might be to trade an asset with a partner company with no intermediary. This is a big goal with many stakeholders.

Build back to a small project that is a minimal viable use case for the technology that clearly articulates added value or savings for your company. Along the same lines as the earlier example, a smaller goal would be to build a private network that can exchange value between trusted parties.

Then build on that value. The next win might be building an instrument that is tradable on your new platform. Each step should demonstrate a small win and value created.

Choosing a Solution

There are three core types of blockchains: public networks like Bitcoin, permissioned networks such as Ripple, and private ones like Hijro.

Blockchains do a few straightforward things:

» They move value and trade value quickly and at a very low cost.

» They create nearly permanent data histories.

Blockchain technology also allows for a few less-straightforward solutions such as the ability to prove that you have a "thing" without revealing it to the other party. It is also possible to "prove the negative," or prove what is missing within a dataset or system. This feature is particularly useful for auditing and proving compliance.

Table 2-1 lists common uses cases that are suited for each type of blockchain.

TABLE 2-1

Table Head

Primary Purpose	Type of Blockchain
Move value between untrusted parties	Public
Move value between trusted parties	Private
Trade value between unlike things	Permissioned
Trade value of the same thing	Public
Create decentralized organization	Public or permissioned
Create decentralized contract	Public or permissioned
Trade securitized assets	Public or permissioned
Build identity for people or things	Public
Publish for public recordkeeping	Public
Publish for private recordkeeping	Public or permissioned
Preform auditing of records or systems	Public or permissioned
Publish land title data	Public
Trade digital money or assets	Public or permissioned
Create systems for Internet of Things (IoT) security	Public
Build systems security	Public

There may be exceptions depending on your project, and it is possible to use a different type of blockchain to reach your goal. But in general, here is how to break down different types of networks and understand their strengths and weaknesses:

>> **Public networks** are large and decentralized, anyone can participate within them at any level — this includes things like running a full node, mining cryptocurrency, trading tokens, or publishing entries. They tend to be more secure and immutable then private or permissioned networks. They're often slower and more expensive to use. They're are secured with a cryptocurrency and have limited storage capacity.

>> **Permissioned networks** are viewable to the public, but participation is controlled. Many of them utilize a cryptocurrency, but they can have a lower cost for applications that are built on top of them. This feature makes it easier to scale project and increase transaction volume. Permissioned networks can be very fast with low latency and have higher storage capacity over public networks.

>> **Private networks** are shared between trusted parties and may not be viewable to the public. They're very fast and may have no latency. They also have a low cost to run and can be built in an industrious weekend. Most private networks do not utilize a cryptocurrency and do not have the same immutability and security of decentralized networks. Storage capacity may be unlimited.

There are also hybrids between these three core types of blockchains that seek to find the right balance of security, auditability, scalability, and data storage for applications built on top of them.

Drawing a blockchain decision tree

Some of the decisions you face while working on a blockchain project within your organization can be difficult and challenging. It pays to take time making decisions that involve

>> **Uncertainty:** Many of the facts around blockchain technology may be unknown and untested.

>> **Complexity:** Blockchains have many interrelated factors to consider.

>> **High-risk consequences:** The impact of the decision may be significant to your organization.

>> **Alternatives:** There may be alternative technologies and types of blockchains, each with its own set of uncertainties and consequences.

>> **Interpersonal issues:** You need to understand how blockchain technology could affect different people within your organization.

A decision tree is a useful support tool that will help you uncover consequences, event outcomes, resource costs, and utility of developing a blockchain project.

You can draw decision trees on paper or use a computer application. Here are the steps to create one for uncovering other challenges around your project:

TIP

1. **Get a large sheet of paper.**

    The more choices there are, and the more complicated the decision, the bigger the sheet of paper you'll need.

2. **Draw a square on the left side of the paper.**

3. **Write a description of the core goal and criteria for your project in that square.**

4. **Draw lines to the right of the square for each issue.**

5. **Write a description of each issue along each line.**

    Assign a probability value to encounter each issue.

TIP

6. **Brainstorm solutions for each issue.**

7. **Write a description of each solution along each line.**

8. **Continue this process until you've explored each issue and discovered a possible solution for each.**

Have teammates challenge and review all your issues and solutions before finalizing it.

Making a plan

At this point, you should have a clear understanding of your goals, obstacles, and what blockchain options you have available.

Here's a simple road map for building your project:

1. **Explain the project to key stakeholders and discuss its key components and foreseen outcomes.**

2. **Write up a project plan.**

   This is a living set of documents that will change over the life of your project.

3. **Develop the performance measurements, scope statement, schedule, and cost baselines.**

4. **Consider creating a risk management plan and a staffing plan.**

5. **Get buy-in and define roles and responsibilities.**

6. **Hold a kickoff meeting to begin the project.**

   The meeting should cover the following:

   - Vision for the project
   - Project strategy
   - Project timeline
   - Roles and responsibilities
   - Team-building activities
   - Team commitments
   - How your team will make decisions
   - Key metrics the project will be measured against

REMEMBER

After you complete your project, you aren't done! Go back and analyze your successes and failures. Here are some questions to ask yourself:

>> Are my key stakeholders happy?

>> Did the project stay on schedule?

>> If not, what caused it to be delayed?

>> What did I learn from this project?

>> What do I wish I had done differently?

>> Did I actually create new value for my company or save money?

TIP

You may want to return to this chapter when you have a deeper knowledge of blockchain technology and you're developing a plan to build a project.

Chapter **3**

Getting Your Hands on Blockchain

Blockchains are very powerful tools and are positioned to change how the world moves money, secures systems, and builds digital identities. If you aren't a core developer, you probably won't be doing any in-depth blockchain development in the near future. That said, you still need to understand how blockchains work and what their core limitations are, because they'll be integrated into many everyday online interactions — from how businesses pay people to how governments know that their systems and data are intact and secure.

This chapter helps you get started in the blockchain world. You'll get acquainted with many of the most important aspects of working with blockchains and cryptocurrencies, yet you'll be working with tools that keep you at a comfortable distance from the intimidating and complex inner workings of blockchains. This chapter also helps you establish the basic crypto accounts that you need in later chapters.

Diving into the Bitcoin Blockchain

The Bitcoin blockchain is one of the largest and most powerful blockchains in the world. It was designed primarily to send Bitcoin, the cryptocurrency. So, naturally, in order to create a message in the Bitcoin blockchain, you must send some Bitcoins from one account to another.

When you send Bitcoins from one account to another, a transaction history is recorded in the Bitcoin blockchain. After a transaction has been entered, the information can't be removed — your message will be around as long as Bitcoin is in existence. This concept of permanence is powerful — it's the most important characteristic of any blockchain.

You have several ways of adding extra little messages inside your transaction, but sometimes these methods don't always produce easily readable messages. In this section, I explain how to build the message directly into the Bitcoin transaction.

Embedding the data into the Bitcoin address ensures that it will be easily readable. You can do this by utilizing a Bitcoin vanity address. Think of a vanity address like a vanity license plate on a car. Six-letter Bitcoin vanity addresses can be obtained for free; longer ones cost money. The longer the vanity address, the more costly it is.

In this project, you create two Bitcoin wallets, add funds to one of them, obtain a vanity address, and send a little Bitcoin between your accounts.

TIP

If you already have a Bitcoin wallet with funds in it, you can skip the first section and use that wallet.

Creating your first Bitcoin wallet

A Bitcoin wallet address is composed of 32 unique characters. It allows you to send and receive Bitcoins. Your private key is a secret code associated with your Bitcoin address that lets you prove your ownership of the Bitcoins linked with the address.

WARNING

Anyone with your private key can spend your Bitcoins, so never share it.

Your first Bitcoin wallet needs to be linked to a credit card or bank account. I recommend using one of the following Bitcoin wallets:

- **Coinbase** (www.coinbase.com)
- **Xapo** (www.circle.com)

To set up your first wallet, just go to one of these URLs and create an account. It just takes a few minutes. When you have your account open, add a little money to it so you can experiment — $5 is a great starting point.

Creating a second Bitcoin wallet

To receive the Bitcoins you'll send, you need to make a second Bitcoin wallet. For this second wallet, don't use a Circle or Coinbase wallet — they don't have the functionality you need for this purpose.

The easiest Bitcoin wallet to use for this project is the Blockchain.info wallet. Follow these steps to create it:

1. **Go to the Blockchain.info website** (`www.blockchain.info`).

2. **Click Wallet.**

3. **Click Create Your Wallet.**

4. **Enter an email address and password.**

Generating a Bitcoin vanity address

A Bitcoin vanity address is like having a personalized license plate for your car. It is a Bitcoin address that has a string of numbers or letters that appeals to you. A vanity address is optional, but a fun way to see your message in Bitcoin. There are a several free ways to create a Bitcoin wallet vanity address. My favorite is BitcoinVanityGen.com. To create your vanity address using BitcoinVanityGen.com, follow these steps:

1. **Go to the BitcoinVanityGen.com website** (`www.bitcoinvanitygen.com`).

2. **Enter six letters into the Type Letters field.**

Bitcoin only allows for small messages, and your vanity address will make up the content of your message, which you can easily read in Bitcoin.

TIP

Choose something cool because you can reuse your address whenever you want after it has been created.

3. **Click Generate.**

4. **Click Email.**

5. **Enter your email address.**

BitcoinVanityGen.com emails you when your vanity address has been found.

6. **Click the link in the email from BitcoinVanityGen.com.**

You'll be given your new vanity address and the private key associated with the address.

7. **Copy your address and private key, and keep them in a safe place.**

You will need your address and private key for the next section.

WARNING

Never share your private keys! Save your private key and a public key someplace safe. Use your public key to receiving or send Bitcoins. (You can share your public Bitcoin keys as much as you want.) The private key is the actual keys to your Bitcoins. If your private key is stolen or lost, you've lost your coins forever.

REMEMBER

Cryptocurrency is unforgiving. Start off with small amounts of money when you're learning how to use these systems.

Transferring your vanity address

In this section, you transfer your vanity address to a wallet. Transferring it will allow you to manage your address, and send and receive Bitcoins easily. Follow these steps to get started :

1. **Log into your Blockchain.info wallet (see "Creating a second Bitcoin wallet," earlier in this chapter).**

   Figure 3-3 shows The settings page at blockchain.info.

2. **Click Settings and then click Addresses.**

3. **Next to Imported Addresses, click Manage Addresses.**

   The screen shown in Figure 3-1 appears.

FIGURE 3-1: Managing your addresses.

4. **Click Import Address, enter your private key, and click Import.**

   You've now created an address that allows anyone to read your vanity address when you send or receive Bitcoins.

Making an entry into the Bitcoin blockchain

Now that you have two Bitcoin wallets, you can make an entry into the Bitcoin blockchain. You do that by sending Bitcoins between your two wallets. Here's how (the specifics vary from one wallet to the next, but this is the general idea):

1. **Log into the Bitcoin wallet that you added the initial funds to (see "Creating your first Bitcoin wallet," earlier in this chapter).**

   It prompts you to enter the recipient.

2. **Navigate to the page where you can send money, and copy and paste your vanity address (see "Generating a Bitcoin wallet vanity address") into the address field.**

3. **Enter a small amount of money that you would like to send, and then click Send.**

Congratulations! You've just sent your first permanent message! You have forever engraved your message into the history of Bitcoin.

If you enjoyed learning how to do this and want to take your knowledge further, you can access a helpful online tutorial on sending Bitcoin messages at www. blockchainpie.com/blockchain-tutorial-bitcoin-message.

TECHNICAL STUFF

A Bitcoin transaction normally takes ten minutes to be confirmed, but could take several hours. The larger the value of the transaction, the longer you should wait. An unconfirmed transaction has not yet been included in the blockchain and is still reversible.

Reading a blockchain entry in Bitcoin

In the preceding section, I show you how to create a small permanent message in Bitcoin. Data on the Bitcoin blockchain is not encrypted because the data needs to be confirmed by the nodes. This means it will be easy to find the message that you created in the last project.

TIP

If you've just made the transfer of Bitcoins between your two wallets, wait about 10 or 15 minutes before following these steps.

1. **Go to the Blockchain.info website (**www.blockchain.info**).**

2. **Enter your vanity address in the Search box and press Enter.**

   The transaction page appears.

That's all it takes to find your transaction and read the massage that you built into the address.

Using Smart Contracts with Bitcoin

A *smart contract* is autonomous software that can make financial decisions. The blockchain world is abuzz about smart contracts because they're both amazing and terrifying in their implications for how the world economy operates.

In simple terms, a smart contract is a written contract that has been translated into code and build as complex if-then statements. The contract can self-verify that conditions have been met to execute the contract. It does this by pulling trusted data from outside sources. Smart contracts can also self-execute by releasing payment data or other types of data. They can be built around many different types of ideas and do not need to be financial in nature. Smart contracts can do all this while remaining tamper resistant from outside control.

Blockchain technology allowed smart contracts to come into existence because smart contracts offer the permanence and corrupt resistances that were once provided only by paper, ink, and a trusted authority to enforce it all. Smart contracts are a revolution in how we conduct business. They ensure that a contract will be executed as it was written. No outside enforcement is needed. The blockchain acts as the intermediary and enforcer.

Smart contracts are a big deal because when machines start executing contracts, it becomes difficult or impossible to undo. It also brings up an important nature of these instruments that can't be overlooked and my first law of smart contracts: *She who controls the data, controls the contract.* All smart contracts verify an external data feed to prove performance and release payment to the correct party.

WARNING

Although smart contracts are a revolutionary new technology, they can't yet interpret the *intent* of the parties entering into the contract. Legal contracts in our society rely on people to interpret what the parties entering into the contract meant. Computers (at least so far) can only understand code, not the intent of the parties.

Building your first smart bond

A *smart bond* is a type of smart contract that can hold and release an object of value on its own, while also monitoring payments in various currencies using spot price data feeds. Many different types of smart contracts exist, and new ones are being invented every day.

Follow these steps to build your first smart bond:

1. **Go to the SmartContract website** (www.smartcontract.com).

2. **Click Sign Up.**

   The Sign Up page appears.

3. **Enter an email address and password and click Create an Account.**

   SmartContract sends you an email with a confirmation link.

4. **Click the link in the email sent to you by SmartContract to verify your account and log in.**

5. **Click Create Contract.**

6. **Click the Smart Bond tab (see Figure 3-2).**

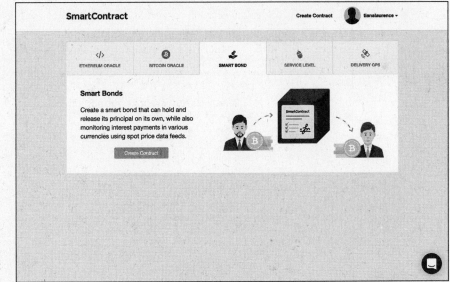

FIGURE 3-2: The Smart Bond tab.

7. Click the Create Contract button.

You're ready to build your first if-then statement.

8. Click the Smart Terms tab.

Smart contracts verify an outside data feed to prove the performance of your contract and trigger the release of payment. Here you choose the conditions that will trigger your smart contract.

9. Choose Performance Monitoring.

Performance monitoring will look to see if an action has been taken outside of the contract. In your case, this will be the movement of funds from one account to another.

10. In the If Payment To field, enter one of your Bitcoin addresses (created earlier in this chapter).

11. In the Is field, enter a small dollar amount that you would like to transfer from one Bitcoin address to the other.

12. In the By Expiration Date field, enter a date a few days from now.

This sets the time parameters that the contract will use to monitor outside sources.

13. Click the Description tab (see Figure 3-3).

FIGURE 3-3: The Description tab.

14. **In the Smart Contract Title field, enter a name for your contract.**

15. **In the Brief Description field, enter — you guessed it! — a brief description of the contract.**

    The description should act as a brief summary of the agreement's purpose. Here you can also attach a legal document or other data, such as a image.

16. **Click the Attachments section.**

    WARNING

    Smart contracts are new technology and can have hiccups. It is best to only attach things that are unimportant and that you'd be okay exposing publicly.

17. **Click Attach Documents.**

    You can attach an image or a PDF.

18. **Click the Sign & Send tab.**

19. **In the Address field, enter your email address to send yourself the contract.**

20. **Click the Finalize Contract button.**

    Now your contract will be monitoring the Bitcoin blockchain to monitor whether you send funds to the Bitcoin wallet address that you listed earlier.

21. **Return to your Bitcoin wallets and send funds between the two wallets.**

    Make sure to use the address and a little more than the amount that you listed on the contract in Steps 10 and 11. When the contract you created sees the record of the transaction of the Bitcoin blockchain, you'll be notified by email.

    REMEMBER

    The Bitcoin network will take a cut of the transaction, so add a little more to it so that it will meet the terms of the contract. For example, if you set the contract to $5, send $5.15 just to be safe.

Checking the status of your contract

You can check the status of your contract at any time by following these steps:

1. **Log into your SmartContract account at** www.smartcontract.com.

2. **Go to your Contract Dashboard.**

    After your transaction has been completed, the contract will show as complete. Your contract status is located below the Contract Dashboard.

REMEMBER

Give the Bitcoin network 10 to 15 minutes to process your transaction before checking the status of it.

Building a Private Blockchain with Docker and Ethereum

Private blockchains hold the promises of both having the benefits of a private database and the security of blockchains. The idea is most appealing for two reasons:

>> **Private blockchains are great for developers because they allow them to test ideas without using cryptocurrency.** The developers' ideas can remain a secret as well, because the data has not been published publicly.

>> **Large institutions can capitalize on the security and permanence of blockchain technology without their transactions being public the way they are in traditional blockchains.**

TIP

Most of this book assumes you're just learning about blockchain for the first time and have little to no programing skills, but this section requires some knowledge of GitHub, Docker, and how to use your computer's terminal. If you need a quick recap on coding before you dive in, I recommend *Coding For Dummies* by Nikhil Abraham (Wiley) for a great overview on coding for nontechnical people. If you don't plan to ever be hands-on with blockchain technology, you might want to skip the rest of this chapter.

In this section, you dive into building your first blockchain. You build it in two steps. The first step is to prepare your computer to create your private blockchain. Don't worry — it's made easier with tools from Docker and work that has been done by talented developers on GitHub. The second step is building your blockchain inside your Docker terminal.

Preparing your computer

You need to download some software on to your computer in order to try this blockchain project. Start by downloading the Docker Toolbox. Go to www.docker.com/toolbox to download the correct version for your operating system.

Next, download GitHub Desktop. Go to http://desktop.github.com. After you've installed GitHub Desktop, create a GitHub account at www.github.com by clicking Sign Up and entering a username, email address, and password, and then clicking the Sign Up for GitHub button.

Now you need to create a place to store your blockchain data. Create a folder on your computer's desktop called `ethereum`. You'll use this folder to hold your future repository and other files. Follow these steps to complete the process:

1. **Open GitHub Desktop.**

2. **Sign into the GitHub Desktop application on your computer with your new GitHub account.**

3. **Return to your web browser and go to** `www.github.com/Capgemini-AIE/ethereum-docker`.

You see the page shown in Figure 3-4.

4. **Click the Clone or Download button.**

You'll be given two choices: Open in Desktop or Download Zip (see Figure 3-5).

5. **Select the Open in Desktop option.**

The GitHub Desktop application will reopens.

In the GitHub Desktop application, navigate to the project folder `ethereum` **and click Clone.**

Cloning from GitHub copies the information you need to build your new blockchain. Follow the steps in the next section to get started building your private blockchain.

FIGURE 3-5:
Open in Desktop.

Building your blockchain

You're going to use the free Docker Quick Start Terminal tool to build your blockchain. It gives you access to a virtual machine, cutting down the time required to set up and debug your system. Because of these features, it lets you create a stable environment for your blockchain, so you don't have to worry about the settings on your machine, and you can get up and running faster.

Follow these steps:

1. Launch Docker on your computer using the Docker Quick Start Terminal.

   The Quick Start Terminal should be located with your applications or on your desktop.

   The Docker application launches a terminal you will use to build your blockchain.

2. Change directories in the terminal to ethereum.

   The files you create making the new blockchain will go into the desktop file you made in the preceding section. You need to give a command to the terminal in order to change directories. If you're on a Mac or running Linux, enter the following command:

```
cd ~ /Desktop/ethereum/ethereum-docker/
```

If you're on a PC, enter the following command:

```
cd ~ \Desktop\ethereum\ethereum-docker\
```

TIP

If these commands don't work for some reason, search the web for tutorials that explain how to change directories for your type of system.

Now you can utilize the Ethereum–Docker files.

3. **Create one standalone Ethereum node by entering the following command into your terminal:**

```
docker-compose -f docker-compose-standalone.yml up -d
```

This one line of code will have created the following:

- One Ethereum bootstrapped container

- One Ethereum container that connects to the bootstrapped container

- One Netstats container with a web UI to view activity in the cluster

4. **Take a look at your new blockchain by opening a web browser and going to** http://$(docker-machine ip default):3000.

Congratulations! You've built your own private blockchain. If you're so inclined, say a word of thanks to Graham Taylor and Andrew Dong, who put a lot of time into creating the Ethereum–Docker integration.

2
Developing Your Knowledge

Discover the beginning of blockchain technology with the Bitcoin blockchain.

Clarify your knowledge of the Ethereum network, and expand your understanding of decentralized autonomous organizations and smart contracts.

Identify the core concepts of the Ripple network and how it exchanges almost any type of value instantly.

Evaluate the Factom blockchain and its ability to secure data and systems.

Dig into the high-speed DigiByte blockchain, and learn about some of the fun applications being built around blockchain technology.

Chapter **4**

Beholding the Bitcoin Blockchain

Warning! After reading this chapter, you may become hooked on this cool emerging technology. Read at your own peril.

Bitcoin demonstrates the purest aspects of blockchain technology. It's the baseline that all other blockchains are compared to and the framework that nearly all have drawn upon. Knowing the basics of how the Bitcoin blockchain operates will allow you to better understand all the other technology you encounter in this ecosystem.

In this chapter, I fill you in on the fundamentals of how the Bitcoin blockchain operates. I offer safety tips that will make your Bitcoin experience smoother and more successful. I also show you practical things you can start doing now with Bitcoin. In these pages, you find out how to mine the Bitcoin token, giving you a new way to get your hands on Bitcoins without buying them. Finally, you discover how to transfer your tokens to paper wallets, and other practical ways to keep your tokens safe online.

Getting a Brief History of the Bitcoin Blockchain

Bitcoin and the concept of its blockchain were first introduced in the fall of 2008 as a whitepaper and later released as open-source software in 2009. (You can read the Bitcoin whitepaper at www.bitcoin.org/bitcoin.pdf.)

The author who first introduced Bitcoin in that 2008 whitepaper is an anonymous programmer or cohort working under the name of Satoshi Nakamoto. Nakamoto collaborated with many other open-source developers on Bitcoin until 2010. This individual or group has since stopped its involvement in the project and transferred control to prominent Bitcoin core developers. There have been many claims and theories concerning the identity of Nakamoto, but none of them have been confirmed as of this writing.

Regardless, what Nakamoto created is an extraordinary peer-to-peer payment system that enables users to send Bitcoin, the value transfer token, directly and without an intermediary to hold the two parties accountable. The network itself acts as the intermediary by verifying the transactions and assuring that no one tries to cheat the system by spending Bitcoins twice.

Nakamoto's goal was to close the large hole in digital trust, and the concept of the blockchain was his answer. It solves the Byzantine general's problem, which is the ultimate human problem, especially online: How do you trust the information you are given and the people who are giving you that information, when self-interest, malicious third parties, and the like can deceive you? Many Bitcoin enthusiasts feel that blockchain technology is the missing piece that will allow societies to operate entirely online because it reframes trust by recording relevant information in a public space that cannot be removed and can always be referenced making deception more difficult.

Blockchains mix many old technologies that society has been using for thousands of years in new ways. For example, cryptography and payment are merged to create cryptocurrency. *Cryptography* is the art of secure communication under the eye of third parties. Payment through a token that represents values is also something humans have been doing for a very long time, but when merged, it creates cryptocurrencies and becomes something entirely new. Cryptocurrency lets you take the concept of money and move it online with the ability to trade value securely through a token.

Blockchains also incorporate *hashing* (transforming data of any size into short, fixed-length values). Hashing also incorporates another old technology called Merkle trees, which take many hashes and squeeze them down to one hash, while still being able to prove each piece of data that was individually hashed (see Figure 4-1).

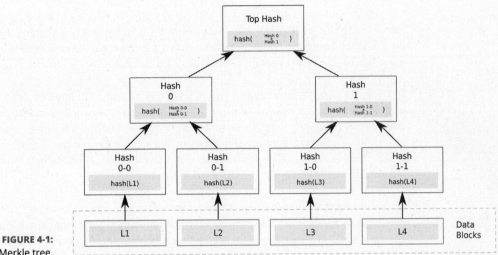

FIGURE 4-1:
A Merkle tree.

Ultimately, blockchains are ledgers, which society has been using for thousands of years to keep financial accounts. When all these old models are merged and facilitated online in a distributed database, they become revolutionary.

Bitcoin was designed primarily to send the Bitcoin cryptocurrency. But very quickly, the creators realized that it had a much larger potential. With that in mind, they architected the blockchain of Bitcoin to be able to record more than the data concerning the movement of the token. The Bitcoin blockchain is the oldest, and one of the largest, blockchains in the world. It's composed of thousands of nodes that are running the Bitcoin protocol. The protocol is creating and securing the blockchain.

REMEMBER

In very simple terms, the *blockchain* is a public ledger of all transactions in the Bitcoin network, and the *nodes* are computers that are recording entries into that ledger. The *Bitcoin protocol* is the rules that govern this system.

Nodes safeguard the network by mining for the cryptocurrency Bitcoin. New Bitcoins are created as a reward for processing transactions and recording them inside the blockchain. Nodes also earn a small fee for confirming transactions.

Anyone can run the Bitcoin protocol and mine the token. It's an open-source project that thrives as more individuals participate in the network. The fewer people who participate, the more centralized it becomes — and centralization weakens the system. The primary thing that makes Bitcoin a secure system is the large number of independent nodes that are globally distributed.

The most successful miners have robust systems that can outperform slower miners. Early in its history, you could run the Bitcoin protocol and earn Bitcoins on a desktop computer. Now, in order to have any hope of ever receiving Bitcoins, you need to purchase expensive specialized equipment or use a cloud service.

In order to create a message in the Bitcoin blockchain, you have to send some Bitcoin from one account to another. When you send a transaction in Bitcoin, the message is broadcast across the whole network. After the message is sent, it's impossible to alter it because the message is recorded inside the Bitcoin block-chain. This feature makes it imperative that you always choose your message wisely and never broadcast sensitive information.

Broadcasting the same message to thousands of nodes and then saving it forever in the token's ledger can add up in a hurry. So, Bitcoin requires that you keep your communications very short. The current limit is just 40 characters.

THE LIMITATIONS OF BITCOIN

Blocks that make up the Bitcoin blockchain are limited to 1MB in size. This limits the number of transactions that the Bitcoin blockchain can handle to seven transactions per second. New blocks occur on average about every ten minutes, but they aren't guaranteed.

These limitations are hard-coded into the Bitcoin protocol and help ensure that the network stays decentralized. And decentralization is key to Bitcoin's robustness. Larger blocks would impose hardships on the miners and might push out small operations.

Bitcoin has built-in limitations that prevent it from handling the global volume of monetary transactions. It is also being used to secure other types of data and systems. The demand to use the secure Bitcoin ledger is high. This difficulty is referred to as *Bitcoin bloat,* and it has slowed down the network and increased the cost of transactions.

At this point, most blockchain developers are only experimenting with expanding the utility of the Bitcoin blockchain. Most are not at a point where they need to scale up their prototypes and concepts so that the Bitcoin blockchain can handle their request. Other new blockchain technologies have also helped bring down the pressure on Bitcoin and given developers cheaper options to secure data.

AS THE WORLD TURNS: THE DRAMA OF BITCOIN

There is significant conflict around the core development of Bitcoin. Dubbed the Bitcoin Civil War or the block size limit debate, the general conflict is between keeping Bitcoin core as it is and enlarging the functionality of the software. This conflict appears simple, but the repercussions are enormous. Bitcoin's permanent nature and the billions of dollars' worth of assets that Bitcoin software secures mean that every code change is rigorously reviewed and debated.

Beyond the internal conflict, Bitcoin is also under intense scrutiny from the outside. The decentralized nature of Bitcoin that may displace central authorities made it a target for regulators. Bitcoin is also favored by people who want to purchase illicit items anonymously or move money from a controlled economy to a noncontrolled economy, bypassing governmental controls. All these factors have given Bitcoin a bad rap and drawn the judgment of society. Entrepreneurs that wanted to capitalize on the technology of Bitcoin rebranded it. The change in terminology was used to differentiate the software structure of Bitcoin and other cryptocurrencies. Software that used the structure of cryptocurrencies began being called *blockchain*. The shift to deemphasize the controversial tokens and highlight the structure of cryptocurrencies changed both government and commercial views of Bitcoin from fear to excitement.

Bitcoin is a living and ever-changing system. The Bitcoin core development community is actively seeking ways to improve the system by making it stronger and faster. Anyone can contribute to the Bitcoin protocol by engaging on its GitHub page (`www.github.com/bitcoin`). However, there is a small community of dominant core developers of Bitcoin. The most prolific contributors are Wladimir Van Der Laan, Pieter Wuille, and Gavin Andresen.

Debunking Some Common Bitcoin Misconceptions

People are often suspicious of anything new, especially new things that aren't easy to understand. So, it's only natural that Bitcoin — a totally new currency unlike anything the world had ever seen before — would confound people, and a few misconceptions would result.

Here are some of the misconceptions you might have heard about Bitcoin:

>> **Bitcoin was hacked.** There has never been a successful attack on the Bitcoin blockchain that resulted in stolen Bitcoins. However, many central systems that use Bitcoin have been hacked. And wallets and Bitcoin exchanges are often hacked due to inadequate security. The Bitcoin community has fought back by developing elegant solutions to keep their coins safe, including wallet encryption, multiple signatures, offline wallets, paper wallets, and hardware wallets, just to name a few.

>> **Bitcoin is used to extort people.** Because of the semi-anonymous nature of Bitcoin, it's used in ransomware attacks. Hackers breach networks and hold them hostage until payment is made to them. Hospitals and schools have been victims of these types of attacks. However, unlike cash, which was favored by thieves in the past, Bitcoin always leaves a trail in the blockchain that investigators can follow.

>> **Bitcoin is a pyramid scheme.** Bitcoin is the opposite of a pyramid scheme from the point of view of Bitcoin miners. The Bitcoin protocol is designed like a cannibalistic arms race. Every additional miner prompts the protocol to increase the difficulty of mining. From a social point of view, Bitcoin is a pure market. The price of Bitcoins fluctuates based on market supply, demand, and perceived value.

>> **Bitcoin will collapse after 21 million coins are mined.** Bitcoin has a limit to the number of tokens it will release. That number is hard-coded at 21 million. The estimated date of Bitcoin issuing its last coin is believed to be in the year 2140. No one can predict what will happen at that point, but miners will always earn some profit from transaction fees. Plus, users of the blockchain and the Bitcoins themselves will be incentivized to protect the network, because if mining stops, Bitcoins become vulnerable and so does the data that has been locked into the blockchain.

>> **Enough computing power could take over the Bitcoin network.** This is true, but it would be extremely difficult, with little to no reward. The more nodes that enter the Bitcoin network, the harder this type of attack becomes. In order to pull this off, an attacker would need the equivalent of all the energy production of Ireland. The payoff of this sort of attack is also extremely limited. It would only allow the attacker to roll back his own transaction. He couldn't take anybody else's Bitcoins or fake transactions or coins.

>> **Bitcoin is a good investment.** Bitcoin is a new and interesting evolution in how people trade value. It isn't backed by any single government or organization, and it's only worth something because people are willing to trade it for goods and services. People's willingness and ability to utilize Bitcoin fluctuates a lot. It's an unstable investment that should be approached cautiously.

Bitcoin: The New Wild West

The Bitcoin world is much like the early days of the Wild West. It's best to approach cautiously until you figure out who the good guys and bad guys are and which saloon serves the coldest beer. If you fall victim to a scam, you'll have little to no protection.

TECHNICAL STUFF

Bitcoins fall within the definition of *commodity* under the U.S. Commodity Exchange Act and are considered a currency in many European countries, but there is little to no oversight.

In this section, I list three of the common scams that are prevalent in the crypto-currency world. They all revolve around stealing your coins and look a lot like traditional cons you might already be familiar with. This list isn't exhaustive, and crooks are nothing if not creative, so be very cautious when using Bitcoins. You never know what's around the next corner.

Fake sites

Websites that look like exchanges or web wallets but are fakes have plagued some of the top Bitcoin websites. This type of scam is common in the Bitcoin world and on the web in general. Scammers hope to make money by stealing login information from users or misleading them into sending Bitcoins.

TIP

Always double-check the URL and only use secure websites (those that start with `https://`) to avoid this problem. If a website or claim seems doubtful, check to see if it's listed on Badbitcoin.org (`www.badbitcoin.org`). This is not an exhaustive list, but has many of the bad players listed.

No, you first!

"Send me your Bitcoins, and then I'll ship you the goods." Smells fishy, right? Scams like this are similar to money wire fraud. In this type of fraud, an individual pretends to sell you something but never delivers.

The semi-anonymous nature of Bitcoins — combined with the inability to do a charge back — make it tough to get your money back. Plus, governments do not currently offer protection for Bitcoin transactions, so you're up that proverbial creek without a paddle.

Fraudsters will try to win your trust by sending fake IDs or even impersonating other people you may know. Always double-check the information they send you.

TIP

The best way to dodge this sort of scam is to listen to your instinct and never put more Bitcoins at risk than you're willing to lose. If there is a way to verify the identity of the person offline, do so.

Get-rich-quick schemes

Crazy get-rich-quick schemes have proliferated the cryptocurrency world. The good news is: It's easy to recognize them if you know what to look for.

Often, you'll be promised massive returns, and there is some kind of recruitment and indoctrination process. This process could include things like sales training, asking you to recruit your friends and family, and promising that this is a risk-free investment and that you'll never lose your money.

The bottom line: If a scheme looks too good to be true, it probably is. No matter what, take a hard look at how the investment is generating value outside of what you'll receive from your investment. If there is no clear and rational reason that a significant amount of value is generation rate, it's a scam.

TIP

Run all investments by a lawyer and a CPA. They can help you understand your risks and tax implications.

Mining for Bitcoins

You can get started earning Bitcoins in a variety of ways. Mining for Bitcoin is how to earn Bitcoins by participating in the network. It's usually handled by special mining hardware that is expensive and specialized. The equipment also needs Bitcoin mining software to connect to the blockchain and your *mining pool* (a collaboration of many miners jointly work together and then splitting the rewards of their efforts).

Here are three standard ways to explore mining Bitcoin:

>> **Bitcoin-QT:** The Bitcoin-QT client is the original software written by Satoshi Nakamoto. You can download it at https://bitcoin.org/en/download.

>> **CGminer:** CGminer is one of the most popular mining software. It is open source and available for Windows, Linux, and OS at www.github.com/ckolivas/cgminer.

>> **Multiminerapp:** The Multiminerapp is an easy Bitcoin client to run. You can download it at www.multiminerapp.com.

REMEMBER

Bitcoin is a very competitive environment, and unless you buy specialized mining equipment, you may never earn any Bitcoins. I don't endorse or recommend any particular mining equipment in this book because the industry is constantly changing and quickly out of date. Expect to pay between $500 and $5,000 per machine on average. Amazon.com is a good place to look. They have a large offering and many customer reviews to help guide you.

Cloud mining allows you to start earning bitcoins in an industrious afternoon, without the need to download software or buy equipment. Just follow these steps:

1. **Go to** https://hashflare.io/panel.

   The return on investment for cloud mining can be negative. Review your option carefully to make sure it is a positive investment.

WARNING

2. **Scroll down the home page and click the Buy Now button under SHA-256 Cloud Mining.**

   When I wrote this book, this option had the highest return on investment and the lowest startup cost. Take the time to reassess this on your own because this might have changed.

TIP

3. **Go through the sign-up process.**

4. **Link your bitcoin address.**

   If you haven't established a bitcoin address, turn to Chapter 3 and follow the directions to create a bitcoin wallet. You'll need to do this in order to claim your mining rewards.

5. **Buy a small amount of mining power.**

   This will allow you to join the bitcoin network.

6. **Join a mining pool.**

   This step allows you to get a faster mining reward than mining on your own. It pools the resources of several miners and then shares the prize between the pool.

Congratulations! Now just sit back and wait for your mining rewards to start rolling (or dripping) in.

Making Your First Paper Wallet

A *paper wallet* is a paper copy of your public and private key for your Bitcoins. Because they're completely offline, paper wallets are one of the most secure ways to hold Bitcoins when done correctly. The advantage is that your private key is not stored digitally, so it isn't subject to hacking. Making a paper wallet is fairly easy. Just follow these steps:

1. **Go to** www.bitaddress.org.

2. **Move your mouse around the screen until the amount of randomness shows 100%.**

3. **Click the Paper Wallet button.**

   This gives the option to create a paper wallet that you can print.

4. **In the Addresses to Generate field, enter 1.**

   You can make several wallets at once, if you need to, but you might as well just start with one to get the hang of it.

5. **Click the Generate button.**

   Figure 4-2 shows a paper wallet I created.

6. **Click the Print button.**

WARNING

Do not let anyone watch you create your paper wallet. This isn't something you want to do at a public computer. Make sure to use a printer that is private and not connected to the Internet so you're not at risk of your private keys being hacked.

TIP

Laminate your paper wallet to make it a little more durable.

FIGURE 4-2:
A paper wallet.

Chapter **5**

Encountering the Ethereum Blockchain

The Ethereum project is one of the most developed and accessible block-chains in the ecosystem. It is also an industry leader in blockchain innovation and use cases. Understanding this technology is important because it's leading the charge in smart contracts and decentralized organizations.

In this chapter, I cover the makeup of Ethereum and explain the new way to build organizations and companies on the Ethereum blockchain. I also go into depth on safety and practical business applications of the Ethereum blockchain. I fill you in on how the project started and where it plans to go.

This chapter sets you up to create your own decentralized organization. I explain how to mine the cryptocurrency on the test net to fuel your projects. After reading this chapter, you'll be able to set up your own Ethereum wallet and trade the token.

Exploring the Brief History of Ethereum

Ethereum was first described in 2013 in a whitepaper written by Vitalik Buterin, who was very active in the Bitcoin community as a writer and programmer. Buterin saw that there was significantly more potential in Bitcoin than the ability to move value without a central authority. He had been contributing to the colored coin effort within Bitcoin to expand the utility of Bitcoin beyond the trade of its native token. Buterin believed that other business and government use cases that require a central authority to control them could also be built with blockchain structures.

At that time, there was a fierce debate about the Bitcoin network being "bloated" by lots of low-value transactions from applications securing themselves against Bitcoin. The main concerns were that additional applications, built on the Bitcoin protocol, would have problems scaling in volume. Bitcoin was not built to handle the number of transactions needed by the applications. Vitalik and many others saw that in order for people to build decentralized applications in the Bitcoin blockchain, either the blockchain would need a massive code overhaul or they would need to build a new blockchain altogether.

Bitcoin had already been well established at that point. It was clear that the kinds of upgrades to core code that were needed were well beyond what was realistically possible. The politics of Bitcoin would stall any changes to the network. Vitalik and his team established the Ethereum Foundation in early 2014 to raise funds to build a blockchain with a programming language built within it.

The initial development was funded by an online public crowd sale during July and August of 2014. The foundation initially raised a record $18 million through the sale of its cryptocurrency token called ether. People have passionately debated whether this sort of crowd sale is illegal because it may constitute an unlicensed security.

The regulatory gray zone has not hindered the project. If anything, the cutting edge nature of the project has attracted more attention and talent to the foundation. Discontented and disenfranchised developers and entrepreneurs from around the world have flocked to the project. Decentralization is seen as the perfect solution to corrupt and oppressive central authorities.

The $18 million raised in the token sale gave the foundation the funds to hire a large development team to build Ethereum. Ethereum Frontier, the first release of the Ethereum network, went live to the public in July 2015. It was a bare-bones software release that only the more technically savvy could use to build their own applications.

Homestead, the current Ethereum software release, was made available in 2016. It's much more user friendly. Almost anyone can utilize the application template available on it. It has intuitive and friendly user interfaces and a large devoted development community.

Metropolis is the next planned Ethereum release. The main difference will be that applications will be fully developed and well tested. It will also feature even easier-to-use applications and have a larger market appeal where even the nontechnical individuals will feel comfortable using it.

Serenity is the last planned phase of Ethereum development. It's where Ethereum will move from a proof-of-work consensus (in which miners compete to create the next block) to a proof-of-stake model. In a proof-of-stake model, nodes are chosen pseudo-randomly with the possibility of being selected increasing based on their stake in the network. Their stake is measured by the amount of crypto-currency in their possession. The main benefit of the change will be the reduction in cost of energy associated with proof of work. This may make it more attractive for individuals to run nodes in the network, which would increase decentraliza-tion and increase security.

Ethereum: The Open-Source World Wide Computer

Ethereum may be one of the most complex blockchains ever built. It has its own *Turing-complete programming language* (a full-functioning programing language that allows developers to build any type of application). The Ethereum protocol can do just about anything that your average programming languages can do, except it's built inside a blockchain and has the added benefits and security that comes with that. If you can imagine a software project, it can be built on Ethereum.

The Ethereum ecosystem is currently the best place to build decentralized appli-cations. They have wonderful documentation and user-friendly interfaces that get you up and running quickly. Rapid development time, security for small applica-tions, and the ability for applications to easily interact with one another are key characteristics of this system.

The Turing-complete programming language is the main feature that makes the Ethereum blockchain vastly more powerful than the Bitcoin blockchain for build-ing new programs. Ethereum's scripting language makes things like Twitter application possible in few lines of code, and extremely secure.

Smart contracts, like the one you create in Chapter 3, can also be built on Ethereum. The Ethereum protocol has opened up a whole new genre of applications. You can take just about any business, government, or organization's processes and build a digital representation of it inside of Ethereum. Currently, Ethereum's platform is being explored to manage *digital assets* (a new class of asset that lives online and may represent a whole digital asset such as a Bitcoin token or a digital representation of a real-world asset such as corn commodities), financial instruments (like mortgage-backed securities), recording ownership of assets such as land, and decentralized autonomous organizations (DAOs), a new way of organizing a business, nonprofit, government, or any other body that needs to come to agreement and work together for common interest. DAOs are built primarily on the Ethereum platform.

Decentralized applications: Welcome to the future

The most revolutionary and controversial manifestation of Ethereum is the self-governing and decentralized application (DAPP). DAPPs can manage things like digital assets and DAOs.

DAPPs were created to replace centralized management of assets and organizations. This structure has a lot of appeal because many people believe that absolute power corrupts absolutely. For those who are fearful of losing control, this type of structure has massive implications.

Etheria (www.etheria.world), a Minecraft-like game, is an interesting example of this technology at work (see Figure 5-1). The game can't be censored or taken down and will exist as long as Ethereum does. When things are created within Ethereum, even if there were good cause to remove a structure or organization, it's practically impossible to do so.

The power of decentralized autonomous organizations

DAOs are a type of Ethereum application that represents a virtual entity within Ethereum. When you create a DAO, you can invite others to participate in the governance of the organization. The participants can remain anonymous and never meet, which could trigger Know Your Customer (KYC) rules (the process a business must go through to verifying the identity of its clients) and anti-money laundering (AML; the laws and regulations designed to stop the practice of generating income through illegal means) compliance issues.

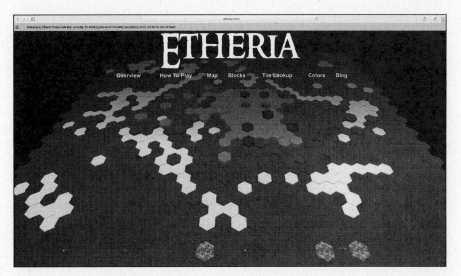

FIGURE 5-1:
The world's first immortal digital game, Etheria.

DAOs have been created for raising funds for investing, but they could also be designed for civic or nonprofit purposes. Ethereum gives you a basic framework for governance. It's up to the organizers to determine what's being governed. Ethereum has created templates for you to help in the creation of DAOs.

Figure 5-2 shows a depiction of the organization of an Ethereum application.

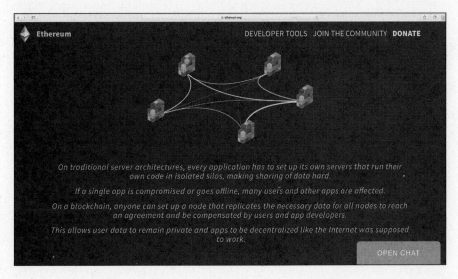

FIGURE 5-2:
Ethereum.org blockchain application depiction.

WITH GREAT POWER COMES . . . GREAT POWER

The first Ethereum DAO ever built is called, confusingly enough, "The DAO." It's an example of some of the dangers that come with decentralized and autonomous entities. It is the largest crowdfunded project in the world — its founders raised approximately $162 million in 26 days with more than 11,000 members. What people had thought was the greatest strength of The DAO became its greatest weakness. The immutable code within The DAO locked into place how the organization would be governed and how funds would be distributed. This allowed the members to feel secure in their investment. Although the code was well reviewed, not all the bugs had been worked out.

The first significant threat to Ethereum came from the hack of The DAO. An unexpected code path in The DAO's contract allowed any sophisticated user to withdraw funds. An unknown user managed to remove about $50 million before he could be stopped.

The Ethereum community debated bitterly about whether it could or should reclaim the ether. The DAO hacker had not technically done anything wrong or even hacked the system. Fundamentalists within the Ethereum community felt that code was law and, therefore, nothing should be done to recover the funds.

The very thing that made Ethereum strong was also its greatest weakness. Decentralization, immutability, and autonomy meant no central authority could decide what to do quickly. There was also no one to punish for the misuse of the system. It really did not have any consumer protection measures. It was a new frontier, like the software name suggested.

After spending several weeks discussing the problem, the Ethereum community decided to shut down The DAO and create a new Ethereum. This process is called *hard forking*. When the Ethereum community hard-forked the network, it reversed the transaction the hacker had committed. It also created a two Ethereums: Ethereum and Ethereum Classic.

Not everyone was in agreement with this decision. The community continues to use Ethereum Classic. The tokens for Ethereum Classic are still traded but have lost significant market value. The new Ethereum token still hasn't regained its old high from before the hack.

The decision to fork rocked the blockchain world. It was the first time a majority blockchain project had hard-forked to make whole an investor. It called into question many of the principles that make blockchain technology so attractive in the first place.

Here's how DAOs basically work:

1. A group of people writes a smart contract to govern the organization.

2. People add funds to the DAO and are given tokens that represent ownership.

   This structure works kind of like stock in a company, but the members have control of the funds from day one.

3. When the funds have been raised, the DAO begins to operate by having members propose how to spend the money.

4. The members vote on these proposals.

5. When the predetermined time has passed and the predetermined number of votes has accrued, the proposal passes or fails.

6. Individuals act as contractors to service the DAO.

Unlike most traditional investment vehicles, where a central party makes decisions about investments, the members of a DAO control 100 percent of the assets. They vote on new investments and other decisions. This type of structure threatens to displace traditional financial managers.

DAOs are built with code that can't be changed on the fly. The appeal of this is that malicious hackers can't monkey with the funds in a traditional sense. Hackers can still find ways to execute the code in unexpected ways and withdraw funds. The immutable nature of a DAO's code makes it nearly impossible to fix any bugs once the DAO is live in Ethereum.

Hacking a Blockchain

Ethereum has never been hacked. The hard fork in 2016 due to the DAO hack mentioned in the "With great power comes . . . great power" sidebar was not an actual hack of the system, but confusingly is often referred to as a hack. Ethereum worked perfectly. The problem was it was too perfect. It became necessary to restart the system when a large amount of money and a majority of its users were threatened.

The only way to correct an action on a blockchain like Ethereum is to do a *hard fork*, which allows for a fundamental change to the protocol. A hard fork makes previously valid blocks and transactions invalid. Ethereum did this to protect the funds that were being pulled out of the first DAO by a user. The DAO hack was conceptually, one of the largest bug bounties ever.

That said, many scams and hacking attempts occur in the cryptocurrency space. Most of these attacks target centralized exchanges and applications. Many hackers want to steal cryptocurrency. It has real value and isn't protected in the same ways that regular money is protected by governments. The anonymous nature of cryptocurrency also makes it appealing to crooks. Catching and prosecuting these individuals is difficult. The cryptocurrency community is fight back, however, and creating new measures to protect themselves.

REMEMBER

Hacking one place is significantly easier and cheaper than trying to overcome a decentralized network. When you read about hacking in the blockchain world, it's likely just a website or a cryptocurrency wallet that has been hacked, not the whole network.

Understanding smart contracts

Ethereum smart contracts are like contractual agreements, except there is no central party to enforce the contract. The Ethereum protocol "enforces" smart contracts by attaching economic pressure. They can also enforce implementation of a requirement if it lives within Ethereum, because Ethereum can prove certain conditions were or were not met. If it doesn't live within Ethereum, it's much harder to enforce.

WARNING

Ethereum smart contracts are not yet legally enforceable and may never be because the perception is that you don't need outside authorities enforcing agreements. Legal systems are controlled by governments. As they stand now, governments are central authorities — some with more or less consent and democratic principles. Within an Ethereum smart contract, each participant has an inalienable vote.

Ethereum smart contracts do not include artificial intelligence. This is a cool possibility in the near future. But for now, Ethereum is just software code that runs on a blockchain.

Ethereum smart contracts are not safe. The DAO hack is a great example of the type of dangers that can occur. It is still early days, and putting a lot of money into an unproven system isn't smart. Instead, experiment with small amounts until all the bugs have been worked out of new contracts.

Discovering the cryptocurrency Ether

Ether is the name of the cryptocurrency for the Ethereum blockchain. It was named after the substance that was believed to permeate all space and make the universe possible. In that sense, Ether is the substance that makes Ethereum possible. Ether incentivizes the network to secure itself through proof-of-work mining, like how the token Bitcoin incentivizes the Bitcoin network. Ether is needed to execute any code within the Ethereum network. When utilized to execute a contract in Ethereum, Ether is referred to as *gas.*

Executing the code within a smart contract also costs some amount of ether. This feature gives the token added utility. As long as individuals want to use Ethereum for applications and contracts, ether will hold a value beyond speculation.

The wild growth in the value of ether has made it a popular token to speculate on. It's widely traded on exchanges around the world. Some new hedge funds are looking at it as an investment vehicle. However, the volatile nature and low market depth make ether a risky investment.

Getting Up and Running on Ethereum

In this section, I walk you through how to get started in the Ethereum blockchain ecosystem. Before you can build anything on Ethereum, you need an Ethereum wallet.

REMEMBER

Your wallet will hold your Ethereum tokens call *ether.* Ether is the cryptocurrency that allows you to create smart contracts inside Ethereum. This is sometimes referred to as *gas.*

Downloading the Ethereum wallet can take some time, but the interface is very intuitive and the instructions provided throughout the process are easy to follow.

TIP

Within the Ethereum wallet, you can win test ether to build your test contracts and organizations. You don't need to mine ether to learn how it works.

Mining for ether

Ethereum is kept running by a network of computers all over the world that are processing the contracts and securing the network. These computers are sometimes referred to as *nodes,* and they're mining crypto Ether.

In order to reward individuals for the time and cost involved in mining, there is a prize of five ethers about every 12 seconds. The prize is given to the node that was able to create the latest block in the Ethereum blockchain.

All new blocks have a list of the latest transactions. The proof-of-work consensus algorithm guarantees that prizes are won most often by nodes with the most computational power. Computers that aren't as powerful can win, too — it just takes longer. If you want to try your hand at mining ether, you can do it with your home computer, but it will take a very long time to successfully mine a block and win ether.

WARNING

Mining ether is not for the technical novice. You need to be familiar with command line. If you don't have a clue what command line is, you probably want to skip this process. Also, be sure to follow the most up-to-date instructions on the Ethereum GitHub (http://github.com/ethereum).

Setting up your Ethereum wallet

To set up your Ethereum wallet, follow these steps:

1. **Go to** www.ethereum.org.

2. **Click the Download button.**

TIP

   You have to scroll down the page a bit to find the button.

   Be sure to save the Ethereum wallet download someplace you can find it later.

3. **Open the Ethereum wallet.**

4. **Click Use Test Net.**

   Here you get set up to mine test ether. This process is much less time-consuming then real ether mining, but it still takes some time.

5. **Create a strong password.**

   Don't forget to save your password someplace safe.

6. **Click through the startup menu.**

   The Ethereum team has a few tutorials that are interesting to review while you're waiting on your test net to download. The download may take ten minutes or so.

7. **Choose Develop ⇨ Start Mining.**

   Don't skip this step. You need the ether for later projects.

You've just set up your wallet, and you're earning test ether for your future smart contract projects.

Building Your First Decentralized Autonomous Organization

DAOs will change how the world does business in the future. They allow anyone in the world to create a new type of company online that is governed by pre-agreed-upon rules that are then enforced through the blockchain network. Creating a DAO is easier than you might think. In this section, you build your first test DAO. I break this project into three sections: build, congress, and governance.

REMEMBER

In order to successfully complete your test DAO, you need to have set up your Ethereum wallet and done some mining on the Ethereum test net (see the preceding section).

Follow these steps to create your first test DAO:

1. **Go to** www.ethereum.org/dao.

2. **Scroll down the page to the Code box (shown in Figure 5-3) and copy the code.**

3. **Open the Ethereum wallet you made earlier.**

    You'll develop your DAO in your Ethereum wallet.

FIGURE 5-3:
The Code box.

Test net and congress

The next phase of your DAO project is setting up the framework for your DAO. Follow these steps:

1. **In your Ethereum wallet, choose Develop ⇨ Network ⇨ Test Net.**

2. **Click the Contracts tab and then click Deploy Contract.**

    The Ethereum team has set up a few test templates for DAOs.

3. **Paste the code you copied in the preceding section into the Solidity code box.**

4. **From the Contract Picker, choose Congress.**

5. **Pick some variables when prompted to do so.**

   Here are your options:

   - The *minimum quorum* for proposals is the fewest votes a proposal needs to have before it can be executed.

   - The *minutes for debate* is the shortest amount of time, in minutes, that needs to pass before it can be executed.

   - The *margin of votes* for a majority. Proposals pass if there are more than 50 percent of the votes plus the margin. Leave it at 0 for a simple majority.

Governance and voting

Now you're going to name and set up the governance of your DAO. You need to set up a *minimum quorum* for proposals (how many votes a new proposal needs to have before it is passed). You also set up the *margin of votes for a majority* (how many votes a plan needs to pass) and the time allotted for discussing new plans.

1. **Name your new DAO.**

   This is kind of like naming a company.

2. **For Debate Times, select 5 minutes.**

   This is how long new proposals are open for conversation.

3. **Leave Margin of Votes for Majority set to 0.**

   This sets up how the democracy of your contract works.

4. **Confirm the price of the DAO.**

   You've mined some Ether in the test net via your wallet when you first set up it up. If you skipped that step, go back and do it now. You need a little of the test net Ether to build your DAO.

5. **Click Deploy and type your password.**

   The DAO may take some time to deploy. When you arrive at your new dashboard, scroll down, and you'll be able to see your DAO being produced.

6. **Click the New icon.**

   A new unique icon will generate that represents your DAO.

Congratulations! You've created your first DAO.

Uncovering the Future of DAOs

Smart contracts and decentralized organizations hold a lot of promise. The pure democratic and hyper-rational nature of them is very appealing. However, at this point, there are more possibilities then knowns, and each contract that is created could be groundbreaking or a massive flop.

If you approach Ethereum as the new frontier that it is, you'll have more success. The Ethereum network has more benefits than drawbacks if you're careful. But expecting everything to work flawlessly and all the participants to act with integrity will open you up to greater losses. Ethereum has its share of bandits, not to mention those friendly enthusiasts who would like you to succeed.

The smart contract hacks of 2016 have highlighted the importance of security and properly reviewing contracts. It also illustrated that there are people with integrity that who fight to fix issues.

Reading this book is only the beginning. It will give you a sound bases to build your knowledge of Ethereum, but as with all new technologies, Ethereum is quickly evolving. Keep reviewing best practices and security measures.

In the following sections, I mention some things to keep in mind as you build your first few DAOs, build smart contracts, and debug your new blockchain systems.

Putting money in a DAO

Don't trust large sums of money to untested and contracts and contracts that haven't been fully vetted. Large contracts are more often targeted by hackers. The DAO hack described earlier in this chapter (see the sidebar "With great power comes . . . great power") showed that even well thought-out contracts have unexpected weaknesses.

REMEMBER

Although, smart contracts and blockchains let you conduct business with anyone around the world, it's still the early days. You can mitigate your risk by working only with known and trusted parties.

TIP

The security landscape will constantly be evolving with new bugs. Reviewing all new best practices is imperative. Manage the amount of money you're putting at risk and roll out contracts slowly and in phases. Ethereum is a new technology, and mature solutions are not yet built.

Building smarter smart contracts

Smart contract programming requires a different mind-set than standard contract writing. There is no third party to make things right if the contract executes in a way that you didn't expect or intend. The immutable and distributed nature of blockchains makes it tough to change an unwanted outcome.

REMEMBER

Your contract will have flaws and may fail. Build safety valves into your contracts so you can respond to bugs and vulnerabilities as they come up. Smart contracts also need an off switch that let you pull the plug and pause your contract when things are going wrong.

TIP

If your contract is big enough, offer bug-hunting bounties that incentivizes the community to find vulnerabilities and flaws in your contract.

As with many things, the complexity of your contract also increases the likelihood of errors and attack vectors. Keep your contract logic simple. Build out small modules that hold each section of the contract. Creating a contract in this manner will help you compartmentalize any issues.

Finding bugs in the system

Don't reinvent the wheel by building your own tools such as random number generators. Instead, leverage the work that the community has already done and that has been well tested.

WARNING

You can only control for things within your own contract. Be cautious of external contract calls. They can execute malicious code and take away your control.

The Ethereum community has an excellent known bug list and even more helpful tips on how to build secure smart contracts on its GitHub page at https://github. com/ethereum/wiki/wiki/safety.

Chapter **6**

Regarding the Ripple Blockchain

R ipple is the one of the most interesting blockchains for moving and trading value globally. The Ripple protocol allows for the fungibility of any type of asset — even between two unlike assets and in nonliquid markets. It does all this at extremely low cost, with exceptionally high security, and in record time. The Ripple infrastructure is being implemented as the framework for new modern banking and trading.

This chapter looks at the important nuances of the technology behind the Ripple blockchain. I explain the finer point of how Ripple is revolutionizing banking and fintech globally. I also fill you in on the practical uses of the Ripple blockchain and specific safety tips for working with Ripple protocol.

This chapter prepares you to trade many different types of value globally. Here, you discover why this technology is important for your industry and how to get started using the Ripple protocol today. You also find out how to set up an account that trades on the Ripple protocol and scams to avoid when operating in this ecosystem.

TIP

If you aren't looking for a large-scale solution for a corporation that is exempt or can obtain a banking license, you may want to skip this chapter because Ripple primarily servicing financial institutions.

Getting a Brief History of the Ripple Blockchain

The Ripple project is older than Bitcoin. It has gone through several iterations, but the original implementation was created by the Canadian developer Ryan Fugger in 2004. Fugger's first iteration was a decentralized monetary system that allowed individuals and communities to set up their own money.

Jed McCaleb, Arthur Britto, and David Schwartz later add to Ryan's work through a company called OpenCoin. Their work helped add more blockchain-like features such as a digital currency system in which transaction chains are published by consensus among members of the network.

Chris Larsen, the first CEO of Ripple, was the founder of several companies including E-Loan and Prosper, both of which were disruptive organizations that changed the consumer lending market. He joined Ripple in August 2012 and led it until 2016.

Ripple has since grown to be a large venture-backed startup. It has some of the biggest names in the investing world backing them, Google Ventures and Andreessen Horowitz just to name a few. As of 2016, Ripple had raised more than $93 million in venture funding. Ripple is also politically active and sits on the Federal Reserve's Faster Payments Task Force Steering Committee and co-chairs the W3C's Web Payments Working Group. It has offices in San Francisco, New York, London, Luxembourg, and Sydney. Many of the founding team have since left Ripple and started new projects.

Ripple has been very disruptive in the banking industry and has seen substantial pushback for its efforts. In 2015, FinCEN fined Ripple $700,000 for Secrecy Act violations. The fine was for selling XRP to Roger Ver, a well-known Bitcoin investor, and failing to file a suspicious activities report because Ver has a felony conviction for selling fireworks on eBay. After the fine, DBS Bank and the Oversea-Chinese Banking Corporation Limited began refusing banking services to Ripple Singapore. It is believed that this happened because these banks felt that issuing assets on blockchains posed more regulatory risk than reward for them. Since then, Ripple has shifted its focus to primarily serving global and regional banks.

Today Ripple is a global financial settlement solution that enables banks and consumers to exchange value. Similar to Bitcoin, the Ripple protocol lowers the total cost of settlement by allowing users to transact directly and instantly. It's built on a distributed open-source Internet protocol, uses a blockchain, and has a native currency called *ripples.*

Ripple's distributed financial technology enables users to send real-time international payments across its networks. Using Ripple, global markets can meet demand for fast, low-cost, and on-demand global payment services.

Ripple is particularly good at cross-border payments and exchanging value between two unlike things. Ripple has created a global network of financial institutions, market makers, and consumers. You can now exchange just about any type of value anywhere in the world and instantly. Ripple is the new foundation for the *Internet of Value.* The idea behind the Internet of Value is that value such as money, cars, land, and commodities can all live and be traded completely online and without intermediaries that facilitate the process. Protocols, such as Ripple, facilitate the trade and fill in the role of intermediary.

Ripple: It's All About Trust

Ripple is an exchange network and a trading platform with a blockchain backend. Institutions use the protocol to clear transactions through Ripple's distributed ledger. They can also settle obligations through Ripple's distributed funds exchange.

There are two main ways to interact on the Ripple network:

>> The financial users of the system participate in the network by issuing, accepting, and trading assets to facilitate payments.

>> The node operators participate in the network by keeping track of transactions and coming to consensus about the validity and ordering of those transactions with the other nodes in the network.

TIP

The terms *node* and *computer* are often used interchangeably. Both terms refer to the machines and code that are used to run the network.

A financial participant must trust the issuers of assets they hold, and a node operator must trust the other nodes in its validator list not to collude to block valid transactions from being confirmed. It is all about trust and aligned incentives for cooperation.

The Ripple network finds a trusted path to exchange all the different types of value within its distributed network. The cryptocurrency for Ripple, XRP, is used to facilitate trade between unlike things of values that have a low trading volume or no trusted path. Between the nodes, the network, and the financial participant,

Ripple has built the basic infrastructure that optimizes the modern payment process and exchanges globally.

In this section, I cover the core functions that the Ripple protocol enables for the banking industry.

There are two critical functions the Ripple network provides:

>> **It acts as a common ledger to connect banks and payment networks.**
This allows banks and payment networks to clear transactions in five seconds. It also gives users continuous connectivity between each other, and has constant monitoring of the flow of transactions across the network.

>> **It acts as a neutral transaction protocol.** Ripple transfers value bilaterally for the same type of value. For cross-currency transactions, Ripple sources funds from its marketplace of liquidity providers. This is a big deal, because liquidity is a major problem for many markets.

Banks are very excited about this technology because it allows them to move away from intermediaries and clearinghouses to a faster, cheaper, and less risky system. Banks have dramatically sped up the process of cross-border payments by removing the need for paper and intermediaries.

Ripple also helps banks reduce risk and cut operational costs of foreign exchange operations by enabling them to directly transact with other banks globally and sourcing liquidity from Ripple's open marketplace of third parties.

The main advantages Ripple offers are the following:

>> Real-time payments

>> Comprehensive transaction traceability

>> Near-instant reconciliation

>> The ability to convert almost any type of currency, commodity, or token

Seeing How Ripple Differs from Other Blockchains

Ripple, like Bitcoin, is neutral and decentralized software. Almost anyone can use Ripple as an open standard to facilitate connectivity and interoperability.

Ripple is significantly different from Bitcoin in its structure and the way the network operates. Ripple is finding the most efficient exchange route, structuring transactions as debts, and using its cryptocurrency as the exchange mechanism between the different types of value that are traded on the Ripple network.

Ripple is all about trust, whereas other blockchains, for the most part, are about trustless systems. In Bitcoin, any two parties can send one another Bitcoin tokens and the network then validates that no one is cheating in that transaction. Part of the way Bitcoin balances every block of transactions is to check to make sure that all the tokens involved have only been spent once.

Another significant difference is that Ripple does not use proof-of-work consensus. The Ripple team has eliminated the large power burden needed by most blockchains to secure themselves. In doing so, Ripple uses significantly less electricity and is faster than traditional blockchains. You can dive deeper into how Ripple works by checking out the whitepaper at `https://ripple.com/files/ripple_consensus_whitepaper.pdf`.

Ripple works very differently from other blockchains. One of the most noteworthy differences is how the network is decentralized and comes to consensus. The nature of decentralization in Ripple is subtle. A node can put any other nodes it wants into its validator list in order to listen to what transactions those nodes want to confirm. The only requirement is that there is sufficient overlap between each node's validator lists, so the network doesn't accidentally come to multiple different consensuses.

Ripple manages that by having each node maintain its own validator list, including Ripple's own nodes. This ensures that there is sufficient overlap. As a node's network grows, the node's list will include more and more validators from well-known trustworthy and independent institutions around the world. Over time, Ripple's consensus process will become more and more decentralized.

Beyond how decentralization and consensus work on Ripple, here are some other important ways in which Ripple differs from Bitcoin:

>> **Ripple is in the middle.** Ripple is software that acts as middleware between financial products and institutions. If you plan to use the Ripple network, you'll likely need to be a licensed money services provider or mobile money operator.

The Bitcoin protocol is open for anyone to utilizes as he or she sees fit. Regulation may change, but at this time, you don't have to be licensed to use Bitcoin.

Any developers can get up and running on Ripple, but using the Ripple software may be illegal if you aren't licensed to do so. This is one of the reasons that Ripple targets large financial institutions as their users. Bitcoin can be used by everyone, and it's specifically useful for small transactions.

» **Ripple is based on a consensus algorithm rather than mining.** It uses probabilistic voting among trusted nodes. This type of consensus allows the nodes to come to agreement and confirm transactions in five seconds. With Bitcoin, a transaction may take hours.

» **Assets inside of Ripple, except XRP (the native token of Ripple), exist as debts.** Bitcoin on the other hand only accounts for the transfer of the Bitcoin token between Bitcoin addresses. Outside markets assess the value of the Bitcoin token.

» **The supply of XRP is set at 100,000,000,000, and Ripple owned and created all 100 billion XRP units at the outset of the network.** They then distributed the XRP to owners of the company and others.

Bitcoin creates new Bitcoin tokens every time it creates a new block. The new tokens are awarded to nodes that win the blocks during consensus. Over time, the supply increases. Algorithmically, Bitcoin is set to stop making new Bitcoins when it hits 21 million.

» **Ripple protects itself from spam and denial-of-service attacks by requiring a minimum transaction cost.** The standard transaction fee is 0.00001 XRP, which is called ten drops.

The Ripple protocol will increase the number of drops required, if higher-than-normal transaction volumes are seen. This is similar to how Bitcoin protects itself from spam, but there is no minimum fee. Bitcoin miners will probably ignore your transaction and it won't be confirmed without including one.

» **XRP does not need a "trust path" to be traded.** Because of this, it facilitates trade when there is no path between two parties. You would need to do an XRP exchange in the middle to facilitate the trade with untrusted parties or low-liquidity markets.

Bitcoin on the other hand is a trustless system. It allows any two parties to trade, even if the parties don't know or trust one another — but the trade is limited to the Bitcoin token. This extra feature in Ripple allows users to exchange just about anything.

» **Ripple picks the nodes used to secure their consensus system for their network.** It isn't quite as open as Bitcoin, where anyone can participate fully in the network. This means that Ripple is somewhat centralized, but it will become more decentralized over time.

Unleashing the Full Power of Ripple

Ripple has stopped opening new consumer wallet accounts on Ripple Trade, its consumer-facing portal. For the most part, Ripple has also pulled down all its consumer-facing products. The regulatory burden of servicing consumers was too high and was clarified by the Financial Crimes Enforcement Network (FinCEN) ruling regarding the need for participants in the virtual currency arena to register as money services businesses under federal law.

The network growing out of the consumer-facing portal wasn't going to rival the growth in the banking network for Ripple. As of now, Ripple is focusing its efforts on servicing large enterprise customers. Banks are the ones who truly need what Ripple can offer at a scale that is profitable for them.

As a consumer, you can access Ripple through third parties. The wallet that Ripple references is GateHub.

The GateHub wallet stores all your different currencies; allows you to send money; and allows you to trade gold, silver, XRP, and Bitcoin on the Ripple network directly from your wallet. It also shows you the net worth of your different currencies as they fluctuate with the market.

GateHub will require you to identify yourself, and setting up your account will take some time. When your account is up and running, you'll be able to explore the power of the Ripple network.

Follow these steps to get up and running on GateHub:

1. **Go to** www.gatehub.net.
2. **Click Sign Up.**
3. **Enter your email address and a password, and click Sign Up.**
4. **Save your recovery key in a safe place.**
5. **Verify your email.**
6. **Verify your identity.**

   GateHub verifies your identity and asks for your phone number, a name, a photo, and supporting documents.

   After you provide your personal information, GateHub will clear your account and you'll be set to trade through the Ripple protocol.

   At this point you can send funds to your new account from your Bitcoin wallets.

If you want to build anything on Ripple, you'll need to be a programmer or at least have access to one. Ripple has great documentation and a support team to get you started.

WARNING

Ripple is made for moving money faster and cheaper. This area of the economy is very heavily regulated. Ripple states clearly that it's only software that enables you to perform these tasks. It's completely up to you to understand and comply with regulations.

If you're still interested in building a custom project on the Ripple network, they'll offer you support. The best way to get started is by going directly to the Ripple build page (https://ripple.com/build/). If you want to dive even deeper into the Ripple network, check out its GitHub at https://github.com/ripple.

Exercising Caution with Ripple

REMEMBER

Ripple, like other blockchains, which work through cryptocurrencies, has many dangers. Use common sense while working in the cryptocurrency world, and follow all other security best practices described in this book. It truly is the new wild west, full of opportunity and risk.

WARNING

Here are some risks unique to Ripple:

>> **Unethical trading:** As described earlier, Ripple was created to move value across the world cheaper and faster than any another network. The structure of Ripple works with clusters of markets. These markets have trusted nodes confirming transactions together. There are small price differences between these groups at times, and these price differences attract unethical trading.

>> **Transaction manipulation:** The Ripple network, in particular, is prone to *arbitrage* (the simultaneous buying and selling assets in different markets in order to take advantage of differing prices for the same asset) because it has many currencies and multiple markets, and clever programmers can manipulate the order of transactions. The two known forms of this on Ripple are as follows:

• **Advantageous arbitrage transaction placement:** Taking advantage of a price difference between multiple markets before the ledger closes. The ledger closes every five seconds, so traders use arbitrage bots to exploit the market. These bots strike a combination of matching deals that capitalize on the small imbalances between the markets and also push their transactions into an optimal position within the ledger. The traders then profit by taking the difference in price of these markets.

- **Large trade front running:** The structure and latency in Ripple's consensus exposes the network to a new type of front running of large trades. It is possible to do this because each node in the network broadcasts transactions to other trusted nodes. During this time, bots will be monitoring all transactions for opportunities to jump in front of large trades.

  The bot will buy up initial offers to fulfill the large purchase and then upsell them to the original owner. At the same time, the bots will also reposition the transactions within the ledger to allow this to happen. The net result of this behavior is that the original owner will receive less value in the trade.

  You can find out more about this vulnerability at `http://available imagination.com/exploiting-ripple-transaction-ordering-for-fun-and-profit/`.

Ripple is excellent about keeping exploits out of its network and has an open offer for programmers to earn money through hunting down bugs, exploits, and vulnerabilities. It is highly likely that these two bugs will be fixed in the near future.

Chapter **7**

Finding the Factom Blockchain

The Factom blockchain is a powerful tool that will help industry scale blockchain technology. It's different from other public blockchains and has unique properties that make it ideal for publishing data streams and securing systems. The Factom blockchain also has a corporation behind it — Factom, Inc. — which spearheads its development and builds tools and products on top of the protocol.

Factom software is being built into systems that govern identity and security of both people and things. They're integrating and bridging other blockchains and blockchain technology as well. The linking between blockchains improves the security of Factom and makes the other blockchains more interoperable.

This chapter explains how Factom works, fills you in on its unique properties, and provides easy-to-follow instructions that will help you get started using it. After reading this chapter, you'll understand many of the core concepts of Factom blockchain technology and know where it will add value to your blockchain projects.

This may be the time to mention that I am a co-founder of and the chief marketing officer at Factom, Inc. Although my aim is objectivity, my enthusiasm for Factom is hard to hide.

A Matter of Trust

Blockchains at their core are about allowing different entities to cooperate and collaborate without needing to trust each other's data security or business processes. Historically, trusted middlemen or industry consortiums have enabled this to happen, but those have high overhead costs and merely shift the trust to a different party. Blockchains shift the trust to a network of disimpassioned third parties and, ultimately, math.

Factom, Inc., is a company that builds blockchain software on top of the open-access Factom blockchain. Factom's recordkeeping software works at a high level by publishing encrypted data or a cryptographically unique fingerprint of that data to the Factom blockchain (shown in Figure 7-1). Additional measures are taken to secure the network by publishing a hash of the whole Factom blockchain every ten minutes in multiple other public blockchains. This extra publishing feature makes Factom different from most public blockchains.

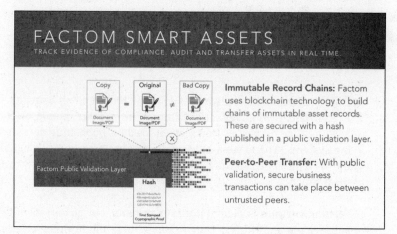

FIGURE 7-1:
The structure of the Factom blockchain.

Illustration courtesy of Factom, Inc.

The concept of the protocol was presented as a whitepaper in 2014 to address scalability issues of Bitcoin. As decentralized applications began securing themselves in Bitcoin, it became clear that entering data into the Bitcoin blockchain was prohibitively expensive at scale, and the Bitcoin couldn't handle high transactional volumes. There was no way to metaphorically get 10 pounds of data into the 5-pound Bitcoin bag.

The Factom protocol was designed to address the cost and volume limitations of other blockchains. The primary objective was to secure data and systems. Because of this objective, Factom is often described as a *publishing engine*. It allows users to write data to its ledger for a small fee. These entries are limited to 10 kibibytes and have a fixed cost that is less expensive and has more capacity for transaction volume by an order of magnitude compared to blockchains that use proof of work.

An important concept to understand is that the Factom blockchain is built in layers and chains. The layers have to do with how the data is structured. They use Merkle trees to leave cryptographic proof that any given data was published within Factom. The cryptographic proof, called a *Merkle root* (32 random characters that can represent a whole tree of individual data), is then published into other public blockchains like Ethereum. This is redundant security that other blockchains don't offer.

TECHNICAL STUFF

A Merkle tree is a mathematical tree constructed by hashing paired data and then pairing and hashing the results until a single hash remains, known as the Merkle root. This cryptographic proof was named after Ralph Merkle in 1979.

Organizing data into chains helps with scalability. Chains allow applications to only pull the data that they're interested in from the Factom blockchain, without needing to download the full data set. How they work is very simple: You can publish your data into an existing chain within Factom, or you can create a new chain. The chain ID is then used in the subsequent items you publish as a way to trace back the data you care about.

The purpose of the Factom blockchain: Publishing anything

Factom is a publishing platform. At its core, it was designed to publish and validate any data. All other tools on it are built around these simple functionalities. Factom can handle transactions that are up to 10 kibibytes; larger transactions need special structuring and require multiple entries. Alternatively, a hash that represents the data can also be published.

Because the Factom protocol is open source, the system acts as a public utility. It's a place where anyone can publish anything and be secured by the Factom blockchain. Not surprisingly, some individuals have published obscene content, but the limit on entry size means they can't publish much. And spam is curbed in the system by charging a small amount per entry. So if you want to swear in the blockchain, it'll cost you.

Factoids are the Factom network cryptocurrency. Decentralized systems need a reward mechanism to incentivize participants. Having this closed system requires cooperation, and builds the long-term network value creation. Factoids can be traded and purchased like any of the other 700 cryptocurrencies on the cryptocurrency market. In the end, Factoids are used to purchase entry credits for the Factom Network.

The cost of an entry is fixed, while the cost of a *Factoid* fluctuates. As a Factoid increases in value, the user can buy more entry credits. This system allows users to be separated from tradable tokens and maintains fixed cost for consumers while allowing for a free market on the speculation of Factoids. This functionality was built into the initial release of Factom to allow heavily regulated industries and governments to utilize blockchain technology without dirtying their hands with tradable tokens.

As of early 2017, the Factom Network sees about 40,000 entries a day. These include things like the Russell 3000 Index and a record of altcoin prices each day. These records are used as historical references and can be utilized as input to smart contracts or to prove history.

Storing and accessing of data today is mostly a solved problem in the industry. Computer backups can be replicated and archived on a massive scale. A big problem that remains is determining which document is the most recent revision, especially across different organizations. With a blockchain-based document management system, organizations can ensure that they're using the same documents as their partners.

Incentives of federation

Many blockchains, such as Bitcoin and Ethereum, use a "proof of work" consensus. In this kind of a blockchain, the consensus algorithm is how a blockchain comes to agreement on new data entered into the system. The consensus system examines whether new data is valid. Public blockchains need a robust system because anyone can add data to a blockchain. Their consensus mechanism is the rule set that determines what makes a block valid and what chain should be trusted.

Proof of work has many characteristics that make it very attractive. It can often require a capital investment into specialized computer hardware and access to electricity (the cheaper, the better). This means that the only requirement to join as an authority in the system is to burn electricity with commodity hardware. It also means that in order to rewrite history, an equivalent amount of energy must be re-burned. This expense makes rewriting history unprofitable and, thus, unlikely.

Proof of work is excellent at securing blockchains. On the other hand, it consumes vast sums of energy and is expensive to operate. It's a cannibalistic arms race where the fastest computers win, and each additional gigahash added to the network increases the challenge.

The more data contained in each block, the more difficult it is to validate. Proof-of-work systems like Bitcoin also requires the full blockchain to validate a specific data point in the system. For others to prove the transaction you made in the Bitcoin blockchain is valid, they must have all of Bitcoin's blockchain downloaded. Currently, that takes several days.

Factom steps back from the question, "Is an entry valid?" The question instead is, "Has the entry been paid for?" The users of the system are the ones validating entries. Factom also structures data in subchains that can be parsed individually to prove the validity of any entry without downloading the full blockchain.

Figure 7-2 shows a diagram of the Factom chain structure.

Illustration courtesy of Factom, Inc.

FIGURE 7-2:
The Factom chain structure.

Factom has been structured this way for commercial applications because members of one industry don't need to download all the irrelevant data about an unrelated industry. For example, verifying that all documents related to a mortgage have been accounted for does not also require downloading years of stock exchange history.

The Factom blockchain also spreads itself out to secure its network against data corruption. Every few minutes, it creates a small anchor into Bitcoin and Ethereum. This does two key things:

» **First and most important, it prevents the servers building the Factom blockchain from undetectably rewriting history.** Because the servers can't control Bitcoin or Ethereum, any history they had recorded is permanent.

» **It prevents the Factom servers from showing two different versions of the blockchain to different people.** Personal customization of web pages is something that Amazon and Facebook routinely do. Showing conflicting histories of business transactions to different companies is a recipe for misunderstanding. Because there is only one Bitcoin blockchain, that prevents altered versions of history from being created.

THE CRAZY EIGHT

Factom, Inc., began as a project to scale Bitcoin and moved into an enterprise software company that builds applications and products for government and large institutions. The company formed by the Factom team had eight original founders that came from a mixed background of sales, development, and engineering.

This is an unusually large founding team that needed a different way of governing, dividing responsibility, and distributing equity. They adopted *holacracy,* a management structure that closely resembles the decentralized networks that they build. Authority and decision-making are distributed among managers. The consensus is created weekly through a 45-minute management meeting.

The company is headquartered in Austin, Texas, and has global projects that involve identity, document management, real estate, and the Internet of Things (IoT). In each case, Factom is working on the record keeping and sharing. It has a partnership with Smartrac, a manufacturer and supplier of radio-frequency identification (RFID) products and IoT solutions, to secure *breeder documents* (documents, like birth certificates, that enable people to get other documents, like Social Security cards or driver's licenses) and prevent identity theft. It's working on IoT security and identity with the Department of Homeland Security and medical record management with the Gates Foundation.

Building on Factom

Factom was created for applications to be built on top of it. It's built for scale, speed, and low cost. It was created to take to the security of the Bitcoin blockchain and make that permanence available to more than what can fit in its limited space.

Authenticating documents and building identities using APIs

Factom has come out with a set of application programming interfaces (APIs) that can be used by development teams to manage and authenticate documents and build identities for people and things. You still need a developer to help you, and they're designed for enterprise integration, not ideal for a small project at this point.

There are two core offerings for the general public:

>> **Apollo:** Apollo is your publish and authentication option. It allows users to feed massive amounts of data into Factom and then refer to it as needed, historically. It would be an ideal place to publish an archive of your website or updates to your protocols, for example.

>> **Iris:** Iris is the platform used to build an identity. It's the underlying technology behind the IoT identity project for the Department of Homeland Security. It builds on the Apollo platform for record management.

You can use the APIs without needing to set up a blockchain or run a cryptocurrency wallet. It takes the headache out of the process and is ideal for those who are worried about the regulatory gray zone that cryptocurrency still falls under.

Getting to know the Factoid: Not a normal token

Factom has a unique value token system, which uses something called the Factoid. The Factoid is a digital commodity that is tradable on some exchanges. It isn't a currency in the same sense as Bitcoin. Factoids can be converted by the owner into *entry credits* (nontransferable tokens that are used to purchase publishing power within the Factom network). This transaction is one-way and it can't be undone. Factoids are effectively burned and are removed from circulation.

Factoids fluctuate in price depending on speculation and utility. Entry credits, on the other hand, have a stable price that is maintained at US$0.001. This makes the fees paid to publish a predictable cost.

The Factom team issued some number of tokens during the crowd sale to raise funds for the core Factom development. At this point, the Factom network has not reached full federation of 32 nodes as outlined in the whitepaper. When the Factom networks reaches 32 nodes, the network will begin rewarding federated nodes and audit nodes with new tokens.

Federated nodes are nodes that are elected by the network to maintain consensus and validate transactions. Audit nodes check the honesty of these nodes and will take one of their positions as a federated node if any given federated node goes offline or breaks one of the system rules.

The issuance of new Factoids to the servers coupled with the extinguishing of the Factoids by the users represents a value transfer. The users are effectively paying for the operation of the servers.

Anchoring your application

Blockchain technology has opened the doors for new products and services. The blockchains themselves serve as the base layer that old technology can reinvent itself with or innovation can be built against. Each blockchain has its own unique properties that make it ideal for specific applications.

Factom is particularly good at securing information, but it still has limitations: the size of each entry, and the fact that the more you publish, the more it costs. Factom is ideal for storing large files in a cloud solution and then using pointers within Factom to locate those files for your application.

Factom is primarily being used as a system to manage documents, and data, and build identity. It integrates with other blockchains, and it can be used to create an oracle for your smart contract.

Publishing on Factom

Factom was built by developers for developers. It requires utilizing your terminal and downloading special software to both use your wallet and make entries into the network.

The team at Factom has been working hard to build a robust system first. They have documentation that will walk you through the process and a GitHub repository with all their open-source software for you to review and even contribute to. Efforts have been made to make Factom more individual consumer friendly, but that's still some time away.

TIP

FreeFactomizer is one of my favorite apps built by a Factom fan. It's very simple to use and allows you to check out the basic functionality of Factom without being a developer, opening a terminal, or doing any coding. It creates a hash of data that you enter into a text box or when you upload a file. It then gathers other hashes of documents submitted by other visitors. Every ten minutes, it combines all these hashes into an entry in the Factom blockchain. It offers a simple proof of existence.

REMEMBER

FreeFactomizer is a free service provided by an individual. It costs money to supply this service and may not be available in the future. There is also no warranty of any kind.

To use FreeFactomizer, follow these steps.

1. **Go to** www.freefactomizer.com.

   Figure 7-3 shows the FreeFactomizer home page.

FIGURE 7-3:
FreeFactomizer is a great way to try out the Factom blockchain.

2. **Upload a document to be hashed.**

   Use an unimportant document — one that doesn't contain sensitive information — because this service is not warranted or secure.

3. **Click Factomize the File Signature.**

   You're given a time estimate for how long it will take for the file to be added to Factom.

4. **Wait for the file to be added to Factom.**

It take at least ten minutes for your file to be bundled with other documents and data. When this process is complete, FreeFactomizer will provide you a link back to Factom Explore.

5. **Check the entry by using Factom Explore, a search tool for the Factom database that allows you to look up entries.**

Another option to try is to uploading the document again. It will send back a note like this: "->Signature already registered." This means that they have added it already to Factom.

Congratulations! You've just stored a fingerprint of data in Factom and explored its core functionality.

Building transparency in the mortgage industry

A blockchain document management service, Factom Harmony is the company's first commercial product. It's targeted for mortgage originators, the institutions that issue loans to consumers for homes.

Factom Harmony (shown in Figure 7-4) works by converting various imaging systems utilized by banks into a blockchain vault for documents. It creates and manages entries in real-time as the mortgage is processed. Then it secures a record of the data within Factom, allowing metadata to be shared transparently and points to confidential data between trusted parties.

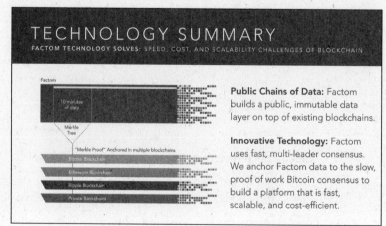

FIGURE 7-4: Factom Harmony.

Illustration courtesy of Factom, Inc.

In simple terms, Factom Harmony is a document catalog that sits on an imaging system. It's a radical improvement over the existing systems because individuals who get involved years later can be sure that the records they're handed are identical to the ones that originated the loan. No longer do mortgage buyers need to trust the fastidiousness of the many intermediaries between origination and themselves.

Factom is hoping to capture some of the value that comes from eliminating costs associated with document assembly. Banks and other originators currently spend immense amounts of time ensuring audits and record reviews are only conducted using the correct set of records and data. This often breaks down when multiple stakeholders coordinate while interacting with loan documents across disparate sources.

Securing data on the blockchain: The digital vault

Factom Harmony (see the preceding section) provides the ability to store the specific data and documents, used for decision and compliance, to a permanent blockchain, while at the same time sharing that data with any party that needs it. Data that has been stored within this system has a clear version history. Missing data is also evident. It was designed for scenarios like audits, lawsuits, foreclosures, loan trading, securitization, and regulatory reviews.

Core technology limitations, during the decade leading up to the 2008 market crash, were focused on speed, throughput, checklist management, and document collection. The systems were not designed to collect records and the associated data in a manner that permanently preserves evidence of the decisions and actions.

Today's regulatory environment requires business to be far more diligent in their efforts to document and maintain the records and data associated with every decisions. Any deficiencies in the documentation of the process are often attributed to malice. Without the ability to perfectly preserve the evidence of the data and the decisions associated with it.

How Harmony works with Factom technology

Factom's technology is a combination of blockchain technology, digital signatures, and a set of cryptographic functions developed by the U.S. National Institute of Standards and Technology (NIST). A series of data points is preserved along with a cryptographic proof on other blockchains that allows users to preserve the data and documents for future use. This process creates an electronic catalog of files that can be accessed and validated at any time by any authorized parties.

Using the SHA-256 cryptographic function, Factom generates a hash of each document and data file stored within the Factom blockchain. The hash creates cryptographic proof that a file has never been altered or changed.

REMEMBER

A *hash* is a kind of "fingerprint" for a set of data that represents the contents of a file but without the risk of the data being exposed.

Additionally, Harmony generates and stores a set of key meta-data points along with the hash for every document and data file associated with the record. Within the metadata documents and data files are associated and linked using the same cryptographic tools. This metadata along with the file hashes is written to the Factom blockchain.

Using blockchain as a public witness

Factom creates multiple public witnesses for the data that it secures. Its blockchain is tiny in comparison to the behemoths such as Bitcoin and Ethereum. Their system does not have mining as part of the consensus mechanism. Currently, the system is not even producing any new tokens. The larger and more decentralized a blockchain, the more secure it is from a successful attack.

Mining cryptocurrency is what most public blockchains do to secure themselves. It's what incentives nodes to join the network.

Factom overcomes this obstacle with a clever method that gives it compounded security. It anchors the data placed in the Factom blockchain within Bitcoin and Ethereum. This is done every ten minutes through hashing. They take the full data set and hash it until there is only one hash that can represent the whole Factom blockchain.

Verifying physical documents: dLoc with Factom

Smartrac, the world's leading developer, manufacturer, and supplier of RFID transponders, inlays, prelaminates, and semifinished cards partnered with Factom. Out of this partnership, a new way of securing physical objects with blockchains was created. This product and service is called dLoc. dLoc was designed as a sticker that can be placed on almost anything. It has special utility for paper-based documents such as breeder documents.

dLoc is an end-to-end secure document management system that uses both hardware and software. dLoc's adhesive Smartrac encoded Near Field Communication (NFC) transponder sticker with an embedded chip is placed on documents or other goods and then secures them using the Factom blockchain.

TECHNICAL STUFF

NFC communication protocols allow two electronic devices, to establish connection when brought near each other.

By combining cloud-based software with Factom's technology, an immutable identity is created over time for just about anything. People with certain levels of clearance can access and validate the physical document using the dLoc mobile app.

dLoc also allows issuing agencies or entities to turn their offline documents into digital instances that can be easily connected to the existing digital systems and bridge the gap between the offline and online worlds. This solution can be applied to a broad range of documents such as birth certificates, land titles, court, and medical records.

dLoc represents the first practical document authentication system that uses the Factom blockchain to solve the data integrity gap between the physical and digital world. It's the first reliable way to secure information on paper-based documents with digital data using blockchain technology. dLoc's data and identity authentication solution hold great promise for both public and private sectors, where paper-based documents are widely used.

REMEMBER

dLoc does not eliminate fraud. People will be people and find ways to bypass, circumvent, and steal. This technology makes it much more challenging and costly to do so. At this point, someone can buy a new identity or forge goods almost anywhere. And in some cases, these identities are indistinguishable from authentic documents and commodities.

dLoc was created as a way to extend the impossibility of blockchain technology to physical objects and documents. They have also created a system that can notify you if your identity is being tampered with and the possibility of doing something about it.

Chapter **8**

Digging into DigiByte

D igiByte is the blockchain that is owning the gaming space. It's a unique system that works well with many interesting applications, from gaming to document management. The team at DigiByte has discovered the right mix of speed, accessibility, and utility for blockchains.

One unique aspect of DigiByte is the five separate algorithms, each of which averages 20 percent of new blocks. This is a big deal because most blockchains are running on just one algorithm, and only the fastest nodes win tokens.

Each of the five DigiByte algorithms accommodates a different type of miner, which has made the DigiByte protocol appealing to more users and increased decentralization. Because of this protocol's approach, attackers would need to gain control of around 60 percent of the total network hash rate to cause any problems. This would entail control of at least 93 percent of one algorithm and 51 percent of the other four (as compared to Bitcoin, which is running one algorithm and is subject to a 51 percent attack). The 51 percent attack concept is one of the greatest weakness of the Bitcoin blockchain. If more than 51 percent of the miners in the Bitcoin network are controlled by one group, they can manipulate the Bitcoin blockchain. If the network is compromised, the token will lose its value and the data secured within the network will be compromised.

This chapter dives into the practical applications and future of the DigiByte block-chain and explains down-to-earth uses for this technology.

Getting Familiar with DigiByte: The Fast Blockchain

DigiByte, also known as the cryptocurrency DGB, is a blockchain that is focused on gaming, payments, and security. The company is headquartered in Hong Kong and was founded by Jared Tate. Tate came from a military and early computer science background and was involved in Bitcoin for many years. After becoming frustrated in the development of Bitcoin core, he launched DigiByte in 2014 and raised a seed round of funding to expand his work in payment and trade.

The DigiByte team has done amazing work that many other projects utilize. Currently, DigiByte is processing 300 transactions per second. To put that into perspective, Bitcoin does about seven transactions per second. The team has many inspiring goals for its project, including match Visa's staggering transaction speed by 2021.

DigiByte is one of the most widely distributed networks, with more than 8,000 nodes in 82 countries. It works similar to Bitcoin in that it can be used to move value between two parties quickly and at a very low cost. It also has some of the same functionality as Bitcoin in that it can secure a small amount of information within its blockchain. Through this mechanism, it allows you to secure data, documents, and contracts at an even faster speed than Bitcoin.

The approachable team at DigiByte has also worked hard to make its project fun. The team offers up prizes for gaming through the platform and tweeting nice things about them. DigiByte has a GitHub and is an open-source project under the MIT license.

DigiByte Gaming, a division of DigiByte is a platform utilizing cryptocurrency within the gaming environment to facilitate a new type of digital advertising. It has a growing user base of more than 10,000. It's a form of permission marketing, where campaigns and incentives drive brand engagement with cryptocurrency prizes and bounties. The ability to do secure micropayments that are nearly borderless gives this type of marketing platform a very interesting competitive advantage.

The borderless engagement allows companies to reach a wider audience. The cryptocurrency also lets companies make payments and offer prizes of just about any size to anyone in the world. It will be exciting to see DigiByte marketing expand beyond the gaming industry.

Mining on DigiByte

DigiByte uses five mining algorithms to process transactions. Each algorithm accounts for 20 percent of all blocks created on the network. This system makes DigiByte a unique and diverse blockchain.

The DigiByte team saw that there was greater advantage to gain by allowing more types of mining on its platform. In systems that have a single algorithm, only the fastest and latest technology will win. This creates a sort of cannibalistic arms race for technology and speed. Because it allows all different types of machines to successfully win tokens, the DigiByte system is open to greater diversity and participation.

Here is a quick breakdown of the five-algorithm system of DigiByte:

>> **SHA-256** (https://dgb-sha.theblocksfactory.com)**:** You must have ASIC mining equipment to utilize the SHA-256 mining option for DigiByte.

>> **Scrypt** (https://dgb-scrypt.theblocksfactory.com)**:** You can use ASIC mining equipment or GPU to run Scrypt for DigiByte.

>> **Qubit** (http://dgb-qubit.theblocksfactory.com)**:** Qubit is a GPU algorithm to mine DigiByte.

>> **Skein** (http://dgb-skein.theblocksfactory.com)**:** Skein is a GPU algorithm to mine DigiByte.

>> **Groestl** (http://dgb-groestl.theblocksfactory.com)**:** Groestl is a GPU algorithm to mine DigiByte.

The multiplicity of DigiByte's algorithms incentivizes more individuals to participate in mining by lowering the barrier to enter the network successfully. The decentralization that resulted from this diversity has attracted many interesting uses for the network. Cryptocurrency miners will often repurpose outdated Bitcoin mining equipment to use on the DigiByte network where they can still find utility for it.

This section dives into how to gain some of the DigiByte tokens, known as DGB. You can mine the cryptocurrency and use it later.

TIP

If you have old Bitcoin mining equipment, it can be used to earn DGB.

Before mining DGB, you should calculate if mining will be a profitable endeavor. Follow these steps:

1. **Go to** www.coinwarz.com/calculators.

   Here, you find a calculator to estimate the payback time for mining many different cryptocurrencies.

   Figure 8-1 shows the cost and profitability calculator tool from CoinWarz.

FIGURE 8-1:
The cost and profitability calculator.

2. **In the Pool Fees % field, enter** 3.

   This is a high estimate on the cost to participate in a mining pool. It often ranges between 0.5 percent and 3 percent.

3. **In the Hardware Costs (USD) field, enter** 500.

   The cost of specialized mining equipment varies widely. A good average cost estimate is $500.

4. **In the Hash Rate (KH/s) field, enter** 470000.

   This is the estimate of how fast your machine can hash in kilohashes per second (KH/s), or 1,000 hash computations per second. The higher the hash rate for mining on a particular blockchain, the more difficult it is to mine that type of cryptocurrency.

TECHNICAL STUFF

You may also see megahashes per second (MH/s), or 1 million hash computations per second; gigahashes per second (GH/s), or 1 billion hash computations per second; terrahashes per second (TH/s), or 1 trillion hash computations per second; and petahashes per second (PH/s), or 1 quadrillion hash computations per second.

5. **Click Calculate.**

The calculator will give you an idea about the costs and profitability of engaging in cryptocurrency mining.

THE EVOLUTION OF MINING

When Bitcoin began, a desktop computer could be used to mine. However, the increase in the hash rate for the Bitcoin blockchain soon consumed all the system resources of normal computers to keep up.

Blockchains that have reached the hash difficulty of gigahashes are beyond the capacity of your average computer. Even this rate can be prohibitive for many miners. It requires a lot of energy, time, and resource to be profitable. Because of DigiByte's five algorithm system, you can still use a normal computer to earn tokens.

Bitcoin miners discovered that they could adapt the graphical processing unit (GPU) in computer graphics cards to do mining. The GPU gave miners often over 50 times the speed advantage, and the GPU also consumed less electricity, so it was cheaper to run.

In 2011, mining farms started popping up. They used specialized equipment called field-programmable gate array (FPGA) processors. These devices attached to miners' computers using a USB port and used less power than CPU or GPU mining.

The best mining hardware now utilizes application-specific integrated circuit (ASIC). ASIC machines mine at extreme hashing speeds and, from my personal experience, they can be quite noisy. If you choose to buy one, take your time and read the reviews. Also, check to make sure it will have a reasonable payback time and be compatible with what you want to mine.

Signing Documents on DigiByte's DiguSign

DiguSign, created by the DigiByte team, is an interesting alternative to traditional cloud storage and e-signature services. DiguSign takes the basic functionality of these applications and adds the permanence and the verifiability of blockchain technology. It allows you to digitally sign documents and then secure them in the DigiByte blockchain.

The DigiByte team believes that DiguSign will be very valuable to lawyers, health-care providers, and in financial services arenas where it's important to keep a clear version history for contracts and a clear established time line on what documents were provided when and to whom.

TIP

You may be able to link your DiguSign account to your cloud storage providers, such as Google Docs, Dropbox, and OneDrive. Until then, each document must be individually uploaded to DiguSign. DiguSign has a free testing version for this service that allows you to create three free blockchain-backed documents or contracts.

DiguSign is still in early testing, but it already allows you to store, unofficially notarize, and validate digital documents.

TECHNICAL
STUFF

DiguSign publishes a SHA256 hash of your document by embedding the hash into a DigiByte blockchain transaction. That transaction is then secured in the DigiByte blockchain.

To set up your account, follow these steps:

1. **Go to** www.digusign.com **and sign up for a DiguSign account.**

2. **Upload your document to DiguSign.**

   You're given the option for creating a document or contract template.

3. **Choose the option to create a document.**

4. **Configure all the required signatures and other fields on your document.**

5. **Enter the emails of the individuals whom you would like to e-sign your document.**

6. **Select the Secure Final Version option.**

   When all parties have signed the document, you need to send the final version to the DigiByte blockchain by clicking Secure Final Version.

You've created a near permanent fingerprint of your document that you can reference at any time.

Earning DigiBytes While Gaming

DigiByte has made the connection between the gaming community's affinity for digital tokens and blockchain technology. Gamers are familiar with using digital currencies within games, so the DigiByte team believes that it's an easy jump to utilize its cryptocurrency token as a way to incentivize user engagement.

DigiByte has set up options to earn DigiByte tokens by playing games such as Counter Strike, League of Legends, and World of Warcraft. The awards are provided through sponsorships by gaming companies and do not draw on a user's GPU power to mine.

DigiByte has created an interesting opportunity for gaming companies to build in added incentive models to gain new players and retain existing ones. It has also found a clever way for gamers to translate the prizes they win in a digital world into money they can spend in the physical world.

You can earn DigiBytes through the DigiByte gaming website. Every day, DigiByte offers multiple Quests that give you the opportunity to gain what are called *XP*. XP then translate into DigiBytes at a set daily rate. You can play World of Warcraft or any of the other games offered, and get paid DigiBytes for playing.

Then you can trade the DGB token on exchanges, such as Poloniex, for Bitcoin. And you can easily turn Bitcoin into other currencies. There are a few layers of separation, but it's a clear fun path to getting paid!

Getting up and running to earn DigiBytes through gaming is fairly easy. You won't be mining to earn tokens, but you won't need to open command line to get started either. Just follow these steps:

1. **Go to** www.digibytegaming.com.

2. **Create a new account.**

   DigiByte allows for social login, making it fast and easy to set up.

3. **Verify your account.**

   Check your email for the link.

4. **Go to** www.battle.net.

   From here, you can create a profile to link to your DigiByte account. This profile will act as a bridge between World of Warcraft and DigiByte.

5. **Set up World of Warcraft on your computer.**

   If you already play this game, you can connect your game key in this step.

6. **Return to** www.digibytegaming.com.

7. **Click the World of Warcraft option.**

8. **Connect your Battle.net account.**

9. **Open your World of Warcraft application and start playing.**

You're now earning DigiBytes while you play!

3 Powerful Blockchain Platforms

IN THIS PART . . .

Ascertain the largest business blockchain consortium, Hyperledger, and what benefits and impact it will have for your industry and organization.

Understand Microsoft's blockchain efforts and core tools available to you through its network offerings.

Evaluate the IBM Bluemix project and the implications of blockchain technology combined with artificial intelligence.

Chapter **9**

Getting Your Hands on Hyperledger

Hyperledger is a community of software developers and technology enthusiasts who are building industry standards for blockchain frameworks and platforms. Their work is important because they're the main group shepherding the blockchain industry into the mainstream and commercial adoption. Hyperledger is the "safe" deployment platform for enterprise teams.

The organization and their unique project are growing every day. As of this writing, they have more than 100 member companies and have several projects in incubation. Their first few projects include Explorer, a web application to view and query blocks, and Fabric, a plug-and-play blockchain application builder. They also have Iroha and Sawtooth, which are modularized blockchain platforms.

In this chapter, I explore the three key projects that are under incubation at Hyperledger. You get a deep understanding of what the future of commercialized blockchain will be for your company and industry. This knowledge will help you as you explore what technologies to utilize and which to avoid, saving you development time and resources.

Getting to Know Hyperledger: Dreams of a Hyper Future

At the end of 2015, the Linux Foundation formed the Hyperledger project to develop an enterprise-grade and open-source distributed ledger framework. They hoped to focus the blockchain community on building robust, industry-specific applications, platforms, and hardware systems to support businesses.

The Linux Foundation saw that there were many different groups building blockchain technology without a cohesive direction. The industry was duplicating effort and the tribalism was leading teams to solve the same problem twice. The foundation knew from its experiences that if this technology was to realize its full potential, an open-source and collaborative development strategy was desperately needed.

The Hyperledger project is led by Executive Director Brian Behlendorf, who has decades of experience dating back to the original Linux Foundation and Apache Foundation, as well as being a CTO of the World Economic Forum. So it's not surprising that Hyperledger has been well received. Many of the top business and industry leaders have joined the project, including Accenture, Cisco, Fujitsu Limited, IBM, Intel, J.P. Morgan, and Wells Fargo. It has also attracted many of the top blockchain organizations.

R3, a consortium supporting the banking industry, has contributed its financial transaction architectural framework. Digital Asset, the software company, gave the Hyperledger mark and some of its enterprise-grade code. The Factom Foundation is also contributing enterprise-grade code and developer resources. IBM and many other organizations are contributing code and other resources to the project.

Hyperledger's technical steering committees ensure robustness and interoperability between these different technologies. The hope is that the cross-industry, open-source collaboration will advance blockchain technology and deliver billions in economic value by sharing the costs of research and development across many organizations.

Hyperledger is identifying and addressing the important features and requirements missing from the blockchain technology ecosystem. It's also fostering a cross-industry open standard for distributed ledgers and holding open space for developers to contribute to building better blockchain systems.

Hyperledger has a project life cycle similar to that of the Linux Foundation. A proposal is submitted and then the accepted proposals are brought into incubation.

When a project has reached a stable state, it graduates and is moved into an active state. As of yet, all Hyperledger projects are in the proposal or incubation stage. Each of the projects is led by a large corporation or startup. For example, Fabric is led by IBM, Sawtooth by Intel, and Iroha by the startup Soramitsu.

Hyperledger, like many open-source projects, uses GitHub (`www.github.com/hyperledger`) and Slack (`https://slack.hyperledger.org`) to connect with teams working on each of the projects. These are great places to get the latest updates and to check on the progress that these projects are making in development.

Focusing on Fabric

Hyperledger's first incubation project, Fabric, is a permissioned blockchain platform. It works like most blockchains in that it keeps a ledger of digital events. These events are structured as transactions and shared among the different participants. The transactions are executed without a cryptocurrency. An optional resource for you to dive deeper into the subject is at `https://trustindigitallife.eu/wp-content/uploads/2016/07/marko_vukolic.pdf`.

All transactions are secured, private, and confidential. Fabric can only be updated by consensus of the participants. When records have been inputted, they can never be altered.

Fabric is an enterprise solution interested in scalability and being in compliance with regulations. All participants must register proof of identity to membership services in order to gain access to the system. Fabric issues transactions with derived certificates that are unlinkable to the owning participant, thereby offering anonymity on the network. Also, the content of each transaction is encrypted to ensure only the intended participants can see the content.

Fabric has a modular architecture. You can add or take way components by implementing its protocol specification. Its container technology can handle most of the mainstream languages for smart contracts development.

Bitcoin, on the other hand, allows anyone to participate anonymously and the community is always looking for ways to be censorship resistant and to enable those who have been disenfranchised. Bitcoin was also mainly engineered for the movement and security of its cryptocurrency token. For this reason, comparing the best practices of Bitcoin to those of Fabric may be unfair.

Building your system in Fabric

A lot of work has gone into making Fabric accessible, but it's still only approachable by people who are technically savvy.

Hyperledger has detailed several use cases that it'll be gearing its technology toward. You'll be able to use Fabric over the outlined use cases in the near future with intuitive user interfaces. For now, you can develop and test the listed use cases with the help of a core developer.

Diving into chaincode development

Contracts between two parties can be translated into code on the Hyperledger Fabric via Chaincode. Chaincode is Hyperledger's version of Ethereum's smart contract. It automates the agreements made within a contract in a way that both parties can trust.

Chaincode is Turing complete like the smart contracts of Ethereum. Currently, you can have a Java developer build a chaincode contract for you. The Fabric team has prepared some common use cases such as digital currencies and sending text messages as part of the core framework.

The Fabric team is also exploring other interesting business use cases that were not complete at the time of this writing but may be available by the time you're reading this.

Hyperledger is early in development and its projects are about two years behind Ethereum's work. However, each of the projects does have substantial teams and resources devoted to it:

>> **Business contracts:** Hyperledger has come up with ways to have both public contracts and private contracts. Private contracts are between two or more parties and contain confidential information. Public contracts are viewable by anyone who takes the time to search for them within Hyperledger. For example, you might use a public contract to make a public offer to sell a product or as a way to solicit bids on a contract.

The makeup of these contracts is more complex than traditional contracts because arbitration and third-party enforcement are removed. Additionally, the authentication of the individuals participating in the contract is needed. Plus, most contracts are unique and can't be standardized. The more complex the contract, the more places it can be corrupted from its original intent. Hyperledger is working on creating a contract management system to help enhance the scalability of Chaincode.

>> **Manufacturing supply chain:** Supply chain management is an exciting blockchain scheme that is being explored on Fabric. Final assemblers could manage all the component parts and supplies that they used in creating their product. This feature would enable you to be responsive to demands and be able to track back the origin of each part to the original producer. In the case of a product recall, it would be easy to find the culprit or the ability to tell the authenticity of each part before it's utilized.

Fabric requires more development before it's ready for this use case because it will need to be easily accessible to everyone in the supply chain. The Fabric team is working on a standard protocol to allow every participant on a supply chain network to input and to track numbered parts that are produced and used on a specific product.

When it's finished, this use case would allow deep searches to be done on the production of each product at any time. This might be ten or more layers deep in the production of any one item. Consumers could then establish the provenance of any manufactured good that is made up of other component goods and supplies. This may have an interesting social impact on consumption.

>> **Securities and assets:** Securities and other assets are well suited to blockchain because they can automate many of the functions that third parties perform. Fabric will allow all stakeholders of an asset to have direct access to that asset and its makeup and history, bypassing intermediaries that now hold that information. Fabric will also speed up the settlement time on assets to near real time.

>> **Direct communication:** In the future, Fabric could also be used as a place where companies can make public announcements and offers. For example, if a company wanted to raise funds and needed to notify all shareholders of the complete details of the offer in real time, it could. Like the decentralized autonomous organization (DAO) of Ethereum, shareholders can make decisions and execute them. Their decisions will be processed and settled in real time. This will make shareholder meetings and voting much easier and faster.

>> **Interoperability of assets:** In the future, Fabric may also have some of the same functionality as the Ripple network (see Chapter 6). It has imagined use cases where companies could exchange assets in low-liquidity markets by matching demands between multiple parties. Instead of settling for market limits on direct trading between two parties, a chain network connects buyers with sellers and finds the best match across multiple asset classes. Hyperledger looks to be well positioned in the future to trade derivatives. You can read more about this work at `http://events.linuxfoundation.org/sites/events/files/slides/TradingDerivatives_LinuxCon_2016.pdf`.

Investigating the Iroha Project

Hyperledger's Iroha project is building on the work completed in the Fabric project. It's meant to complement Fabric, Sawtooth Lake, and the other projects under Hyperledger. Hyperledger added the Iroha project to incubation because the other projects didn't have any infrastructure projects written in C++. Not having a C++ project severely limited how many people could benefit from the work on Hyperledger and the number of developers who could contribute to the project.

In addition, most blockchain development at this point has been at the lowest infrastructure level, and there has been little to no development work on user interaction or mobile applications. Hyperledger believes that Iroha is necessary for the popularization of blockchain technology. This project fills the gap in the market by bringing in more developers and providing libraries for mobile user interface development.

At the time of this writing, Iroha is a very new project and has not integrated with Fabric or Sawtooth Lake. Hyperledger has plans to expand functionality to work with the other blockchain projects soon. Its iOS, Android, and JavaScript libraries will provide supportive functions like digitally signing transactions. It will be very useful for commercial app development, and it will add new layers of security and business models only possible with blockchain technology.

Introducing Sumeragi: The new consensus algorithm

Blockchains have systems that allow them to first agree on a single version of the truth and then record that agreed-upon truth in their ledger. An agreement system is called a *consensus*.

A consensus is complicated. Grasping the nuances of how and why consensuses act in the way they do is well beyond the scope of this book. It's also far more then you'll ever need as a business professional. What *does* matter for you are the consequences of different consensus mechanisms and how they affect what you're doing on that particular blockchain. I'm highlighting Iroha's consensus, Sumeragi, because it's very different from traditional blockchains.

Here are a few key things that make Sumeragi different:

>> **Sumeragi does not have a cryptocurrency.**

>> **Nodes that start consensus are added into the system by the Fabric member services.** Nodes build a reputation over time based on how they've interacted with the ledger. This is a permission blockchain run by known entities.

>> **New entries are added to the ledger in a unique way.** The first node that starts consensus, called the *leader,* broadcasts the entry to a group of other nodes; those nodes then validate. If they don't validate, the first node will rebroadcast after a predetermined duration of time. The broadcasting element is similar to how Ripple's consensus works.

Depending on your use case for blockchain, Iroha may be positive or negative. If you're worried about censorship, Iroha may not be right for you. In this case, you'll be better off looking at a blockchain that is censorship resistant. If you're worried about other players on the network committing arbitrage, Iroha may also not be right — further investigation is needed. If you want to know all the players in your blockchain, Iroha may be exactly what you're looking for.

Developing mobile apps

TIP

Skip this section if you aren't part of the app development space.

Iroha is built for the web and mobile app developers so they can access the strengths of the Hyperledger systems. The Iroha team saw that having a distributed ledger wasn't useful if there were no applications utilizing it.

Iroha has a development path for the following encapsulated C++ components:

>> Sumeragi consensus library

>> Ed25519 digital signature library

>> SHA-3 hashing library

>> Iroha transaction serialization library

>> P2P broadcast library

>> API server library

>> iOS library

>> Android library

>> JavaScript library

>> Blockchain explorer/data visualization suite

One of the major hurdles of the blockchain industry has been in making systems user-friendly. Iroha has created open-source software libraries for iOS, Android, and JavaScript and made common API functions convenient to call. It's still early in development, but Iroha is a good resource to explore for business use cases.

Diving into Sawtooth Lake

Sawtooth Lake by Intel is another distributed ledger project in Hyperledger. It's focused on being a highly modular platform for building new distributed ledgers for companies.

As of this writing, the release version has software that is only *simulating* the consensus. It doesn't provide security for your project and should only be utilized for testing out new ideas.

Sawtooth Lake does not operate with a cryptocurrency. It maintains the security of the platform by allowing businesses to create private blockchains. These businesses running private blockchains then share the burden of computational requirements of the network. In its documentation, Sawtooth Lake states that this type of setup will ensure universal agreement on the state of the shared ledger.

Sawtooth Lake has taken the basic model of blockchains and turned it on its head. Most blockchains have three elements:

>> A shared record of the current state of the blockchain

>> A way of inputting new data

>> A way of agreeing on that data

Sawtooth Lake merges the first two into a signal process they call a *transaction family*. This model is best in use cases where all the participating parties have a mutual benefit to having a correct record.

Intel has allowed its software to be flexible enough to accommodate custom transaction families that reflect the unique requirements of each business. It also built three templates for building digital assets:

>> **EndPointRegistry:** A place to record items in a blockchain

>> **IntegerKey:** A shared ledger that is used for supply chain management

>> **MarketPlace:** A blockchain trading platform for buying, selling, and trading digital assets

Exploring the consensus algorithm: Proof of Elapsed Time

The consensus algorithm for Sawtooth Lake is called Proof of Elapsed Time (PoET). It was built to run in a secure area of the main processor of your computer, called a trusted execution environment (TEE). PoET leverages the security of the TEE to prove that time has passed by time-stamping transactions.

Other consensus algorithms have some kind of time-stamping element as well. The way they ensure the records have not been changed is through publicly publishing their blockchains as proof that it has not been altered. The published ledger acts as a public witness that anyone can roll back and check. It's sort of like publishing an ad in a newspaper to prove something happened.

PoET also has a lottery system that works a bit differently from other blockchains using proof of work. It randomly selects a node from the pool of validating nodes. The probability of a node being selected increases proportionally to how much processing resources that node contributed to the shared ledger. Measures may be put in place to prevent nodes from gaming the system and corrupting the ledger.

Deploying Sawtooth

Intel has put together some fantastic documentation and tutorials at `https://intelledger.github.io/tutorial.html`. They walk you through the process of setting up a virtual development environment for a blockchain, and they even have one for building a blockchain Tic-Tac-Toe game. You need to be familiar with Vagrant and VirtualBox in order to take advantage of what they have to offer.

TIP

You may also want to review *Coding For Dummies* by Nikhil Abraham (Wiley) prior to trying these tutorials.

Chapter **10**

Applying Microsoft Azure

I n this chapter, you get a preview of the exciting innovations that are taking place inside of Microsoft's Azure platform and how these changes can improve your business's efficiency and create new opportunities for products and services.

This chapter helps you compete for, collaborate with, and service customers in a global economy. Blockchain technology is opening new markets and changing business models. Microsoft is working hard to make it an assessable technology for traditional business.

This chapter also explains innovative blockchain bridges that are being built to allow you to connect and scale your existing systems. You find out how to deploy your own blockchain inside Azure and the keys elements to making a safe and hassle-free transition to blockchain systems for your business.

Bletchley: The Modular Blockchain Fabric

Project Bletchley concentrates on offering architectural building blocks for enterprise customers within a *consortium blockchain ecosystem* (a members-only, permissioned networks for members to execute contracts). Bletchley's blockchain fabric platform is powered by Azure, the cloud computing platform for Microsoft. Project Bletchley addresses the following:

- >> Digital identity
- >> Private key management
- >> Customer privacy
- >> Data security
- >> Operations administration
- >> System interoperability

In Project Bletchley, Azure provides the cloud layer for blockchain, serving as the platform where applications can be built and delivered. It will be availability in 24 regions globally. Azure is combining its traditional products such as hybrid cloud capabilities, extensive compliance certification portfolio, and enterprise-grade security to various blockchains. Microsoft wants to make it easier for the existing clients to quickly adopt blockchain technology, especially in controlled industries such as healthcare, financial services, and government.

Figure 10-1 shows project Bletchley's Blockstack Core v14, a new decentralized web of server-less applications where users can control their data.

FIGURE 10-1: Blockstack Core v14.

Azure will work with several blockchain protocols. They are part of Hyperledger project and unspent transaction output (UTXO)–based protocols. This means that the Azure platform doesn't utilize a cryptocurrency and may be more appealing to enterprise customers. They'll also have integrations with more sophisticated protocols, including Ethereum, that do utilize a cryptocurrency to secure the network.

Cryptlets for encrypting and authenticating

Project Bletchley is built around two ideas:

» **Blockchain middleware:** Cloud storage, identity management, analytics, and machine learning

» **Cryptlets:** Secure execution for interoperation and communication between Microsoft Azure, Bletchley's ecosystem, and your own technology

Cryptlets are built as off-chaincode components, written in any language, executed within a trusted container, and communicated over a secure channel. Cryptlets can be used in smart contracts and UTXO systems, when additional functionality or information is needed.

Cryptlets bridge the gap in security between on- and off-chain execution of programs, operating when additional secure information is needed. They're what lets your customer relationship management (CRM) or trading platform connect with your cloud storage and then be secured with Ethereum, for example.

Bletchley's middleware works in tandem with Cryptlets and existing Azure services, like Active Directory and Key Vault, and other blockchain ecosystem technologies, to deliver a complete solution and ensure the reliable operation of your blockchain integration.

Table 10-1 shows the difference between an oracle and a Cryptlet. from the Devcon 2 presentation on Bletchley.

Cryptlets are built by developers and sold in Bletchley's marketplace. They address many different functionality sets that are essential to building distributed ledger-based applications. The market is growing to meet the demands of customers who need the necessary functionality, such as secure execution, integration, privacy, management, interoperability, and a full set of data services.

TABLE 10-1　**Cryplets vs. Oracles**

	Cryptlets	Oracles
Verification requirements	Requires trust with verification with a trusted host (HTTPS), a trusted Cryptlet key, and a trusted enclave signature.	Requires trust but no formal verification.
Infrastructure	Standard infrastructure. You achieve hardware-based isolation and attestation via enclaves available globally in Azure. Bletchley Cryptlet software development kit (SDK) frameworks (Utility and Contract) are available to help you get started quickly creating and consuming Cryptlets.	Customized infrastructure. You can write and host separately. Establishing trust is difficult. Oracles have been platform specific, and documentation is currently very sparse.
Developer use	Many language options are available, and they are blockchain agnostic.	Tied to their own blockchain and few language options.
Marketplace availability	A marketplace is available for publishing and discovery.	No common marketplace is available for publishing and discovery.

Utility and Contract Cryptlets and CrytoDelegates

There are two types of Cryptlets:

>> **Utility:** Utility Cryptlets provide encryption, timestamping, external data access, and authentication. They create a more sound and trusted transactions.

>> **Contract:** Contract Cryptlets are full delegation engines. They can function as autonomous agents or bots. They provide all the execution logic that a smart contract normally does but outside of a blockchain.

Contract Cryptlets are tied to smart contracts and are created when your smart contract is published. They run in parallel with your virtual machine and have greater performance over traditional smart contracts built inside blockchains because they don't require as much cryptocurrency to execute. They're most attractive to noncryptocurrency blockchains users where chaincode and smart contracts are signed by known parties.

Figure 10-2 shows a depiction of a Cryplet container and the secure communication path to your smart contract.

CryptoDelegates allow Utility and Contract Cryptlets to function. They act as adaptors by creating functional hooks in your smart contract virtual machines. They call the Cryptlet from the code of your smart contract, which in turn creates a secure and authentic envelope for transactions.

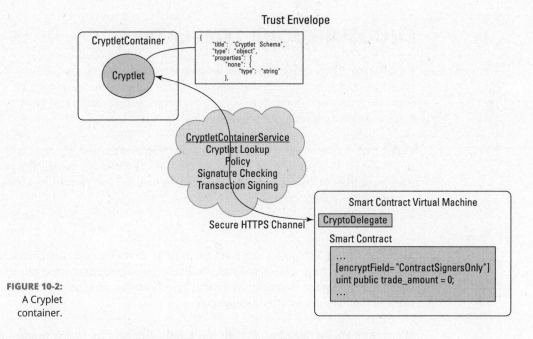

Trust Envelope

{
    "title": "Cryptlet Schema",
    "type": "object",
    "properties": {
        "none": {
                "type": "string"
        },

CryptletContainer

Cryptlet

CryptletContainerService
Cryptlet Lookup
Policy
Signature Checking
Transaction Signing

Secure HTTPS Channel

Smart Contract Virtual Machine

CryptoDelegate

Smart Contract

```
…
[encryptField= "ContractSignersOnly"]
uint public trade_amount = 0;
…
```

FIGURE 10-2:
A Cryplet
container.

Building in the Azure Ecosystem

Azure is a digital ecosystem and cloud computing platform. It connects enterprises directly with their cloud partners and SaaS. This, in turn, allows enterprises to transfer their data in an interconnected, reliable, and secure way.

The Azure cloud platform of Microsoft is the second biggest Infrastructure as a Service (IaaS) platform. It's a reliable and safe haven for your cloud computing and data storage. In Azure, there is a service known as ExpressRoute, which provides consumers a way to directly connect to Azure. This, in turn, prevents the performance and security issues that are widely seen in the public Internet.

In 2015, Microsoft decided to expand its Azure ecosystem using the Ethereum and Hyperledger blockchain systems. The first offering of Azure Blockchain as a Service is powered by Ethereum. Ethereum is a Turing-complete blockchain framework for build applications. Microsoft aims to build more offerings based on the blockchain technology and Hyperledger. It's also growing the Azure marketplace, while transitioning to a portal for customers on Azure.

Microsoft's Azure Stack program incorporates Azure Quickstart Templates, which deploy the various Azure resources with the help of the Azure Resource Manager in order to help you get more work done. The Azure Resource Manger allows customers to work with their business resources as a group. It enables them to deploy, delete, or update all the resources in their solution in a coordinated and single operation.

CHOOSING YOUR TEMPLATE

The Quickstart Template is a tool that is designed to make it easier for the users of Project Bletchley to spin up a private blockchain group. Currently there are about a dozen blockchain templates that allow you spin up blockchain applications in Azure. In the future, more templates will become available.

The Ethereum private version is one of the best at automating the process. step-it is a step-by-step process where you can select the members of the your consortium, determine the number of nodes each user will have on the network, and then geographically distribute those nodes using the Azure cloud to boost resilience.

Azure Quickstart Templates can work for various environments, like production, staging, and testing. Through Azure Resource Manager, customers get several features for tagging, auditing, and security. These features help consumers to manage their resources after deployment.

Microsoft's Project Bletchley is their blockchain architecture that is merged with established enterprise technologies they were already offering. It gives Azure a blockchain backend and marketplace.

Bletchley's ecosystem is an approach taken by Microsoft in order to bring forward blockchain or distributed ledger networks to a wider audience in a safe and effective manner. They want to help build authentic solutions and address actual business problems.

Getting Started with Chain on Azure

Chain, which provides blockchain technology solutions, released its Chain Core Developer Edition on Azure. Chain Core Developer Edition is an open-source and free version of the company's distributed ledger platform. It enables you to issue as well as transfer assets on authorized blockchain networks.

Through its test net, your developers can join or start a blockchain network, access in-depth technical tutorials and documentation, and build financial applications. They can also run their own prototypes on the Chain's test net or create their own personal network on Azure.

Installing Chain's distributed ledger

Chain Core Developer Edition accompanies code samples, a Java SDK, and getting-started guides. In addition, it comes with a dashboard interface and installers for Linux, Mac, and Windows.

Follow these steps to install your Chain Core Developer Edition:

1. **Navigate to Chain's install page at** `https://chain.com/docs/core/get-started/install`.

2. **Choose your operating system from the list.**

3. **Click Download.**

4. **Open the Chain program.**

5. **Run the Chain Core installer.**

Chain has an SDK available that gives you and your developer the software development tools that allows the creation of blockchain applications and assets.

Creating your own private network

You can create a private Ethereum Consortium Blockchain network in Azure. You should be able to do this on your own without the help of a developer. Just follow these steps:

1. **Sign up for or log into your Azure account.**

   There is a free trial option and a pay-as-you-go option that make it easy to try out Azure.

2. **Go to** `https://goo.gl/Ixu5of`.

3. **Click Deploy to Azure.**

   Azure Resource Manager templates are created by members of the Azure community. Microsoft doesn't screen for security, compatibility, or performance.

WARNING

4. **Complete the form.**

5. **Click Purchase.**

Congratulations! You now have a private Ethereum Consortium Blockchain network.

Using financial services on Azure's Chain

Chain launched its open-source and free developer platform. It includes a test network, which is operated by Microsoft, Chain, and the Initiative for Cryptocurrencies and Contracts (3CI). 3CI is the platform launched by Chain, which provides blockchain technology solutions and is Chain Core Developer Edition.

This platform enables you to issue as well as transfer assets on authenticated blockchain networks. It's an effort among leading financial companies and Chain. Various financial applications can be developed via Chain Core.

Many new innovative products are planned to be launched on this platform. The range covers payments, banking, insurance, and capital markets. Additionally, Visa has partnered with Chain in order to develop a secure, fast, and simple way to process business-to-business (B2B) payments worldwide.

Deploying Blockchain Tools on Azure

Azure has several other useful implementations of blockchain technology and tools that you might find useful. I cover four of Azure's core blockchain tools and projects in this section, including its Ethereum implementation; Cortana, an analytics machine learning tool; Azure's data visualization tool, Power BI; and its Active Directory (AD) tool. The last three are not specifically blockchain tools, but they can be used with your Azure blockchain project.

This section gives you an idea of what you can build with Azure and some of the tools available to make your project a success.

Exploring Ethereum on Azure

Ethereum Blockchain is now available as a service on Microsoft's Azure platform. This initiative is offered by ConsenSys and Microsoft in partnership. Solidity is a new project that they created that allows you to start building your decentralized application on Ethereum. Find out more at `https://marketplace.visualstudio.com/items?itemName=ConsenSys.Solidity`.

Ethereum Blockchain as a Service (EBaaS) enables enterprise developers and clients to develop a blockchain environment on the cloud and can be spun up with one click.

When you're deploying Ethereum blockchain on Azure, Azure offers two tools initially:

>> **BlockApps:** A semiprivate and private Ethereum blockchain environment

>> **Ether.Camp:** A built-in developer environment

BlockApps can also be deployed into the public environment of Ethereum. These tools allow rapid development of applications based on a smart contract.

Ethereum is a flexible and open system, which can be customized to meet the varied needs of customers. Read more about Ethereum in Chapter 5.

Cortana: Your analytics machine learning tool

Cortana is a powerful analytics machine learning tool based on cloud systems. It's a fully managed cloud service that enables users to easily and quickly build, organize, and share predictive analytics solutions. It provides many benefits to consumers.

By reviewing the analytics provided by Cortana Intelligence, you can take action sooner than your competitors by predicting the next big thing. This flexible and fast software allows you to build quick solutions for your industry, which are tailored to your particular needs.

Furthermore, the Cortana learning tool is secure and scalable. Cortana offers data value, irrespective of the complexity and size of the data. And, most of all, Cortana allows you to interact with smart agents, so that you can get closer to your consumers in more natural, practical, and useful ways. The Cortana Intelligence Suite is helpful in various sectors, including manufacturing, financial services, retail, and healthcare.

Visualizing your data with Power BI

Power BI, which is offered by Microsoft, is a powerful service based on the cloud system. It covers the latest business intelligence services and tools of Microsoft. This service assists data scientists in envisioning and sharing insights from the data of their organizations.

The Power BI data visualization course, which is provided online by edX, is part of the Microsoft Professional Program Certificate in Data Science. This cloud-based service is rapidly gaining popularity among data science professionals.

Power BI helps you to visualize and connect your data. In this course, students learn how to connect, import, transform, and shape their data for business intelligence. Additionally, the Power BI course teaches you how to create dashboards and share them with business users on mobile devices and the web.

Managing your access on Azure's Active Directory

Azure Active Directory (AD) is a broad access and identity management solution. It provides a wide set of facilities, which allow you to supervise access to cloud and on-premises resources and applications. This includes various Microsoft online services, such as Office 365, in addition to numerous non-Microsoft SaaS applications.

One of the main features of Azure AD is that you can handle access to its resources. These resources can be external to the directory, like Software as a Service (SaaS) applications, on-premises resources or SharePoint sites, and Azure services, or they can be internal to the directory, such as permissions for managing objects through directory roles.

Chapter **11**

Getting Busy on IBM Bluemix

I n this chapter, I introduce you to IBM's blockchain initiatives, which IBM is merging with its other groundbreaking technologies, such as Bluemix, a full Platform as a Service (PaaS) for application building, and Watson, its super computer.

Blockchain technology creates a near-frictionless value exchange. Artificial intelligence accelerates the analysis of massive amounts of data. The merging of the two capabilities will be a paradigm shift that affects the way we do business and secure our connected electronic devices.

If you're involved in the Internet of Things (IoT), healthcare, warehousing, transportation, or logistics industries, you will benefit from the information in this chapter. Also, if you're an entrepreneur and would like to learn about the new capabilities that come with the integration of artificial intelligence (AI) and blockchain on a scalable app platform, this chapter is for you.

Business Blockchain on Bluemix

IBM is now offering blockchain technology that integrates with its traditional offerings, such as IBM Bluemix. Bluemix is an open-standards, cloud-based PaaS for building and managing applications. IBM has integrated a blockchain stack from Hyperledger, which is part of the Lynx foundation and is establishing best practices in blockchain technology.

You'll want to prepare for rapid and fundamental changes within IBM's blockchain initiatives. The technology is very new and still under incubation, both within IBM and Hyperledger.

Hyperledger has several different subprojects in development. As of this writing, IBM is using Fabric, but it may open up Bluemix to other projects. Fabric is open source and under active development within Hyperledger. It's not quite ready for commercial purposes — as of this writing, it's in incubation status.

You can start testing Fabric on Bluemix by using Hyperledger Fabric v0.6. However, IBM warns against running any valuable transactions directly on Fabric v0.6 or any earlier version.

Your isolated environment

Bluemix is the newest cloud offering from IBM. It's an implementation of IBM's open cloud architecture based on Cloud Foundry, an open-source PaaS.

Bluemix enables you to rapidly and easily come up with applications, deploy them, and manage them. Bluemix offers enterprise-level services that can integrate with applications without needing to know how to install or to configure them.

Figure 11-1 shows how IBM relates different aspects of blockchain and IBM systems. You can find out more at `https://goo.gl/12Q6no`.

IBM Bluemix provides four core things:

>> Computing infrastructure based on your apps' architectural needs

>> The ability to deploy apps to a Bluemix public or dedicated cloud

>> Dev tooling, such as code editors and managers

>> Access to third-party open-source tools in their service section

Bluemix gives you everything you need to build your app. It's now offering blockchain infrastructure to test as well.

They have a service for integrating your applications with the Bluemix blockchain. As of this writing, there are two pricing models. A free account gets you what you need to test your idea. You get four peers and a cert authority to sign transactions, as well as a dashboard with logs, controls, and APIs. You also get a few sample apps with source code to experiment with.

FIGURE 11-1:
How IBM Bluemix
and IoT are
merged with
IBM Watson.

The enterprise plan is priced at $10,000 a month and offers higher security and speed than the free model.

Bluemix use cases

Two remarkable entrepreneurial pioneers are using Bluemix and the Hyperledger Fabric integration:

» **Wanxiang:** The largest China-based automotive components company, Wanxiang is working with IBM to deploy a private blockchain. They're embedding property rights into things like electric cars. The goal is to reduce the costs to consumers for leasing equipment. Wanxiang will use its blockchain technology to track the lifespan of the components and refurbish used batteries. Bluemix will take care of everything else.

» **KYCK!:** The financial technology (fintech) startup KYCK! is utilizing IBM's blockchain integration as a novel way to address "know your customer" (KYC) needs for brokerages. This expense is limiting and costly for banks and other financial services. KYC is done to prevent money laundering and illicit trade, and to combat terrorism. KYCK! is building a video conference and encrypted document submissions platform. It will allow brokers to work with and authenticate clients the company has not met in person.

IBM has also built out three simple Chaincode applications that let you play with the IBM Blockchain network:

>> **Marbles:** Marbles is an application that demonstrates transferring marbles between two users. It lets you see how you can move assets on a blockchain.

>> **Commercial Paper:** Commercial Paper is a blockchain trading network implemented on IBM Blockchain. You can create new commercial papers to trade, buy and sell existing trades, and audit the network.

>> **Car Lease:** Car Lease is a lot like the Marbles demo. It's designed to allow you to interact with assets. You can create, update, and transfer. It also allows a third party to view the history.

Watson's Smart Blockchain

IBM's supercomputer, Watson, is also available on the Bluemix platform. Watson is a cognitive computing artificially intelligent computer system. It can analyze structured and, more impressively, unstructured data at incredible speed.

WARNING

This technology is still developing, and customers have complained about its true ability to understand unstructured written language.

Watson can answer questions posed to it through natural language and learn as it absorbs more information. The implication of this technology, when married with blockchain technology, is astounding. One of the first implementations is within the IoT space. There is a strong need to secure data that is emitted from these devices and then make it actionable and intelligent.

Watson's Cognitive computing is simulating human thought processes and using the MQTT protocol. Like a human mind, it grows over time. Its self-learning systems use data mining, pattern recognition, and natural language processing to mimic the way your brain works. Watson processes at a rate of 80 teraflops per second (one teraflop is a trillion floating-point operations). To put this into context, that replicates — and in some cases surpasses — a high-functioning human's ability to answer questions. Watson is able to do this by accessing 90 servers with a combined data store of more than 200 million pages of information, which it processes against six million logic rules. Watson is about the size of ten refrigerators, but it's been getting smaller and faster.

Figure 11-2 shows the how IBM Watson relates different aspects of blockchain and IBM systems. Dive deeper at IBM `https://goo.gl/12Q6no`.

FIGURE 11-2:
How Bluemix
integrates clients,
peers, and IBM
Watson.

IBM is applying these amazing capabilities to IoT data feeds that utilize Chaincode implementation. Chaincode is a Hyperledger smart contract system. Here's how Watson-enabled blockchain for IoT devices will work:

>> IoT devices send data to your private blockchain ledgers for inclusion in shared transactions as a tamper-resistant record marked in time.

>> Partners and third-party service providers can access and supply IoT data as well, without the need for central control and management.

>> All parties can sign and verify data, limiting disputes and ensuring each partner is held accountable for their individual performances.

This is a simple implementation that does not take advantage of all the functionality and capabilities of Watson. Watson's ability to learn and make suggestions, and update out-of-date information will truly make it a powerful blockchain-enabled application in the future.

You can integrate Watson's IoT Platform with Fabric from Hyperledger. This integration allows you to execute Chaincode contracts through cognitive computing oracles. Watson's IoT platform has built-in capability that lets you add selected IoT data to your own private blockchain to create an oracle. This helps you protect the data from being viewed by unauthorized third parties.

When you've established a Bluemix workspace, you can add selective services, including the IoT Platform that integrates several technologies. Fabric is the blockchain technology that provides the private blockchain infrastructure for distributed peers that replicates the device data and validates the transaction through secure contracts.

Watson IoT Platform translates existing device data, from one or more device types, into the format needed by the smart contract APIs. Watson's IoT Platform filters out irrelevant device data and only sends the required data to the contract. Figure 11-3 shows the how IBM Watson integrates with IoT devices and APIs. Watson acts as the Chaincode oracle and allows you to control what information is known to the parties involved in the contract. This functionality is important for privacy.

FIGURE 11-3: The Watson/API/device flow.

Building Your Starter Network on Big Blue

IBM's blockchain technology and IoT Platform offer new promising tools and can be leveraged to address many problems facing companies that are trying to scale:

>> **Security:** The huge volume of data that's collected from millions of devices raises information privacy concerns. Also, hacked IoT devices have been used by nefarious organizations to cripple websites with distributed denial of service attacks.

>> **Cost:** The high volume of messages, data generated by the devices, and analytical processes are going up as more devices come online and utilize that data.

>> **Architecture:** Centralized cloud platforms remain a bottleneck in end-to-end IoT solutions and a central point of attack.

IBM's open-standards-based distributed IoT networks can solve many of the problems associated with today's centralized, cloud-based IoT solutions. Connected devices communicate directly with distributed ledgers. Data from those devices is then be used by third parties to execute smart contracts, reducing the need for human monitoring.

The IBM Watson IoT Platform with a Fabric integration replicates data across a private blockchain network and eliminates the need to have all IoT data collected and stored centrally. Decentralized blockchain networks also improve the security of IoT devices. Unique digital identities are built for each device over time. This new way of creating and securing identity is exceptionally hard to spoof.

These new blockchain identities allow IoT devices to sign transactions that allow smart contracts to execute. A practical application of this would be an insurance product that was fed data from a smart car on the driving behavior of different individuals. The car would send data to be published in Fabric; the insurance product built with Chaincode would then recognize the new data and the identity of your car and update your policy.

The possibilities are nearly endless, and IoT has introduced huge opportunities for businesses and consumers, especially in the areas of healthcare, warehousing, transportation, and logistics.

There are three main tiers of IBM cloud–supported IoT solutions that meet the needs of different IoT business problems:

>> **Devices Gateway:** Device Gateway is for smart devices or sensors that collect data about the physical world. This could be things like weather sensors, temperature monitoring for refrigerated containers, or vital statistics data for a patient. These IoT devices send their data through the Internet for analysis and processing.

>> **IBM Watson IoT Platform:** IBM combines its supercomputer with its IoT Platform to collect data from IoT devices and then analyze the data and take subsequent actions to solve problems. Watson provides machine learning, machine reasoning, natural language processing, and image analysis that enhance the ability to process the unstructured data collected from the sensors.

>> **IBM Bluemix:** Bluemix is an open-standards-based cloud platform for building, running, and managing applications and services. It supports IoT applications by making it easy to include analytical and cognitive capabilities in those applications.

Creating and configuring your IBM Blockchain fabric is easy. You won't even need the help of your developer! Once you've finished configuring your blockchain, you can integrate with the Watson IoT Platform. Follow these steps to have it up and running in a few minutes:

1. **In the Bluemix account dashboard, click Use Services or APIs.**

2. **In the Application Services section of the service catalog, click Blockchain.**

3. **Verify your blockchain selections.**

- **Check your space.** If you have more than the default dev space, verify that you're deploying the service in the intended space.

- **Check your app.** Leave it unbound.

- **Check your service name.** Change the name to something that's easy to remember.

- **Check your selected plan.** Select the free plan.

4. **Click Create.**

Your IBM Blockchain will deploy to Bluemix and give you two peer nodes initially.

There is huge potential for developing cost-saving IoT applications using block-chain. Distributed ledgers with embedded smart contracts can improve security and trust, and automate processes. The IBM Watson IoT Platform can be combined with Bluemix-based blockchain services to provide a ready-to-deploy platform for blockchain-based and open-standards-based, IoT applications.

TIP

The development and testing of these implementations are straightforward but will require the support of a developer.

Follow these steps to set up your first project:

1. **Set up your private blockchain infrastructure on Bluemix.**

You need a developer to set up the integration of your private blockchain based on the IBM Blockchain service.

2. **Develop and deploy smart contracts in the blockchain based on device data.**

An example of this would be to have a contract modify payment of the shipments of goods if it was delivered after its due date.

3. **Connect your devices to the IBM Watson IoT Platform.**

You need to have your developer connect the sensors/gateway to the Watson IoT Platform. When that's done, the IoT devices will send data to be filtered, aggregated, and published to your blockchain.

4. **Integrate your IoT device's data with the blockchain distributed ledger.**

Have your developer integrate the Watson IoT Platform so it can send data to IBM Blockchain services running in Bluemix.

5. **Install your monitoring UI.**

   a. Enable blockchain in the Settings tab.

   b. Configure the connection to the Blockchain service.

   c. Click the Add button and fill in the Blockchain service details in the pop-up dialog box.

   d. Confirm all your changes.

   e. Select the blockchain menu to map the device data. You may need your developer's support here.

   f. Follow the wizard and provide the required inputs to finish mapping the device data to the blockchain contract.

6. **Deployed the Chaincode ID.**

   When the real-time data arrives, smart contracts are executed on the data. Based on the outcome, a transaction is completed and recorded in the digital ledger and then shared with all peers.

7. **Develop client applications for end users.**

   A few challenges need to be overcome on the IBM system and in the early IoT blockchain development. Many IoT devices have limited computing power or are hard to modify. Encrypting and verifying data requires processing power and may cause issues with battery life.

Now you can create your own Chaincode contract. You may need the help of your developer because it requires using GitHub and GoLang. Here's a high-level overview of the process so you can see the needs of this type of project:

1. **Create a GitHub project.**

   This is where you'll store your smart contracts.

2. **Set up a local Hyperledger development and testing environment.**

   You need to install a few things on your computer including Docker, Pip, Git client, Go, and Xcode for Mac users. Review Chapter 3 for instructions on how to set up Docker.

3. **Download the IBM sample smart contracts.**

   This step is optional but will make building your first contract easier.

TIP

4. **Create a test smart contract.**

5. **Build out your contract executables.**

   Your contract must convert an executable. The sample has the contract executables built in.

6. **Test the contract in the Hyperledger sandbox.**

7. **Deploy the contract in GitHub.**

Congratulations! You've set up your IBM contract. You can go back later and map the contract to an IoT device in your Bluemix dashboard.

4
Industry Impacts

Understand the future of the financial services industry when it utilizes blockchain technology to move money around the world quickly and inexpensively.

Clarify your knowledge of global real estate as it relates to blockchain technology.

Identify opportunities in the insurance industry to reduce fraud and increase profits through new insurance instruments.

Examine the large-industry implications of permanent systems within government organizations and legal frameworks.

Clarify other large global trends in blockchain technology and how they'll shape the world you live in and the everyday tools you use.

Chapter **12**

Financial Technology

The first to adopt blockchain technology were banks, governments, and other financial institutions — and they're the fasting-growing blockchain users, too. The powerful tools that are being built to manage and move money will reshape our world in new and unexpected ways, so it makes sense that financial technology (fintech) would jump onboard.

This chapter gives you the inside scoop on what governments are currently doing with blockchain technology and how it will affect you. Fintech touches your life every day, whether you're aware of it or not.

In this chapter, I introduce you to future banking trends, new regulations, and the new tools that can help you move money faster and cheaper. I also explain new types of investment vehicles and other blockchain innovations. Finally, I warn you about potential risks of investments involving virtual currency and new blockchain-technology-enabled financial products.

Hauling Out Your Crystal Ball: Future Banking Trends

Banking was the first industry to recognize the threat of Bitcoin and then the potential of blockchain to transform the industry. The banking sector is highly regulated, and the fees to organize and operate as a bank are expensive. These heavy regulations have been an insulating and protective shield for the whole industry, as well as a burden. The application of fast, efficient, digital money that doesn't carry the cost of handling cash and that is traceable as it moves through the financial system was an intoxicating and threatening proposal. The idea that value can be held outside the control of central authorities also piqued the interest of financial institutions and governments that back currencies.

Initially, these financial institutions and governments tried to squelch blockchain with regulation. Today, they're embracing blockchain through investment across the board.

In 2013 and 2014, the U.S. Securities and Exchange Commission (SEC) issued a warning to investors about the potential risks of investments involving virtual currency. The warning was that investors might be enticed with the promise of high returns and would not be skeptical enough of the new investment space that was so novel and cutting-edge. According to the SEC, digital currency was one of the top ten threats to investors. Today, the SEC stands ready to engage with companies and investors as cryptocurrency gains traction within all industries.

Not even two years later, countries around the world — including the UK, Canada, Australia, and China — began investigating how they could create their own digital currencies, seizing cryptocurrency for themselves and put money on the blockchain. The turning point was when they began to perceive that the benefits started outweighing the risks. Bitcoin had been able to stand up to hackers for several years, even when many government systems were compromised, making it an appealing system to try. Innovations in blockchain technology promised to be able to handle the billions of transaction need to support economies, making a cryptocurrency feasible at scale.

Blockchains are in themselves permanent and unalterable records of every transaction. Putting a country's money supply on a blockchain controlled by a central bank would be utterly transformative because there would be a permanent record of every financial transaction, existing at some level within their blockchain record, even if they weren't viewable to the public. Blockchain technology and digital currencies would reduce risk and fraud and give them ultimate control in executing monetary policy and taxation. It would not be anonymous like Bitcoin was at first. In fact, quite the opposite: It would allow them a full and auditable trail of every digital transaction made by individuals and companies. It might even allow central banks to replace commercial banks' role in circulating money.

The question of what the future for banking will look like can be scary and exciting. Consumers can now pay friends through their phones almost instantly in almost any type of currency or cryptocurrency. More and more retail stores have begun utilizing cryptocurrency as a way to pay for goods and accept payment from customers. In Kenya, using cryptocurrency is more normal than not. But this is still not the mainstream option for most of the world. Western markets are still in the early adoption phase.

Given that most individuals have their wealth locked into legal tender issued by governments or locked into assets that are within existing government systems, fintech innovations must merge with these existing systems before we see the mainstream utility of blockchain or digital currencies. If regulators find ways to tax and register accounts, mass adoption of customer-facing wallets with digitized tokens is two or three years down the road.

The business-to-business market will start utilizing blockchain much quicker. A production-hardened system with the associated policies and operations are less than two years away. Ripple and R3 among others have been hard at work making this possible. These systems will first focus on the institutional creation of digitized representations of deposits. These are IOUs between internal organizational departments and between trusted partners, like vendors. Regulators, central banks, and monetary authorities are all investing heavily in making this possible. Canada and Singapore have been moving very quickly.

Know your customer (KYC) and anti-money-laundering (AML) regulations require banks to know who they're doing business with and ensure that they're not participating in money laundering or terrorism. Banks issuing cryptocurrencies still have significant challenges to overcome first. In order to stay compliant with KYC and AML regulations, they need to know the identity of all the individuals utilizing their currency. In many cases, people's bank accounts are already debit and credit service of transactions, like distributed ledgers in blockchains, except for centralized. The first candidates in this area are going to be regions where regulators, banks, and central banks work together. Singapore and Dubai are good candidates that already have blockchain initiatives.

Moving money faster: Across borders and more

Assessing the transaction volume needed to be met by a blockchain handling the currency of an economy like the UK or U.S. is difficult. The U.S. alone is processing billions of transactions a day and over $17 trillion in value a year. That's a lot of responsibility for a new technology! The nation would be crippled if its monetary supply were compromised.

The International Monetary Fund, the World Bank, the Bank for International Settlements, and central bankers from all over the world have met to discuss blockchain technology. The first step toward faster and cheaper money would be adopting a blockchain as the protocol to facilitate bank transfers and interbank settlement. Official digital currencies that ordinary citizens use on a daily basis would come much later.

Individual consumers wouldn't directly feel the cost reduction from utilizing a blockchain for interbank settlement. The savings would be seen in the bank's bottom line as cost reductions for fees charged by intermediaries.

Consumers will still want retail locations and commercial banks for the foreseeable future. But millennials have already adopted app-activated payments through PayPal, Venmo, Cash, and more. A new way of paying through their phones won't faze them.

The great challenge is that if all money is digital, compromising it could be catastrophic. It's possible that the architecture of blockchain systems would be strong enough. The issue might be instead that the code within the system is executed in an unexpected manner, as happened in the decentralized autonomous organization (DAO) hack on Ethereum (see Chapter 5). If the cryptocurrency were operating on a traditional public blockchain, then 51 percent of the nodes in the network would have to agree to fix the issue. Getting an agreement in place might take a lot of time, and it wouldn't be practical for businesses and people who need stable and secure money at all times.

REMEMBER

Many blockchains operate as democracies. A majority (51 percent) of a blockchain's nodes network are needed to make a change.

Creating permanent history

Data sovereignty and digital privacy are going to be huge topics in the future. Fraud prevention will be easier because if the whole economy is utilizing a cryptocurrency, there will always be an auditable trail inside the blockchain that secures it. This is enticing for law enforcement, but a nightmare for consumer privacy.

From a customer perspective, there's already an audit trail for everything you purchase with a credit or debit card. From an institution perspective, it's a beneficial to have audit trails because it increases transparency of documentation and life cycles of the movements of these assets between different regions. It adds legitimacy to the trading of assets and allows them to bake compliance into their day-to-day transactions.

The "right to be forgotten" rules in Europe, which allow citizens the right to not have their data forever propagated on the Internet, are a difficult challenge for blockchains, because blockchains can never forget. Governments and corporations would have permanent historical records of every transaction, which could be devastating to national security if they were exposed to the public. Or in a company's case, it may allow their competitors to have an inside scoop on how their competitors are investing.

The biggest challenge to using a permissionless blockchain such as Ethereum or Bitcoin would be guaranteeing that you haven't sent money to an OFAC country to support terrorism. The answer is that you can't because there are somewhat anonymous and anyone can open a wallet. It is possible to create algorithms to trace transaction movement — the U.S. government has been doing this for years — but anyone can move value in a permissionless world.

The Office of Foreign Asset Control maintains sanctions on specific organizations or individuals in what are considered high-threat countries. The government is unable to track the history of transactions when using permissionless platforms anonymously.

The need for KYC and AML makes a case for the permissioned blockchain in the shared ledger space. The software company R3 developed Corda, a private and permissioned blockchain-like platform to meet many of these challenges directly. They specifically do not globally broadcast the data from their participants. This keeps the data within the Corda blockchain private and was the primary nonfunctional requirement requested by the more than 75 banks that worked with R3 to adopt blockchain technology. They need to maintain their privacy and meet strong regulatory demands.

Going International: Global Financial Products

Blockchains will usher in many new types of securities and investment products. New markets will be opening with more efficient ways of calculating risk because collateral will be a lot more transparent and fungible across institutions when they accounted for it within a blockchain back system.

Hernando de Soto, the famous Peruvian economist, estimates that by providing the world's poor with titles for their land, homes and unregistered businesses would unlock $9.3 trillion in assets. This is what is meant by the term *dead capital.*

It is imaginable that countries that can free their dead capital, the unfinanceable real property they own, they will be able to bundle and sell these interest in these assets across a global marketplace. This would be things like transparent mortgage-backed securities for new real estate developments in Colombia or Peru.

In the future, countries will be able to free up their dead capital. Owners of properties, undeveloped land, and un-financeable properties will now have the opportunity to sell the interests in these assets across a global marketplace.

These assets will be so appealing because asset managers will be able to actively parse underperforming assets given the transparency and capability of one being substituted in place of another through blockchain-based technology. The use of blockchains to manage these assets will give managers the power always to own top-performing securities, removing the rotten apples, reclassifying them, and selling them as new securities.

For non-institutional customers, micro-investments will be an attractive outlet enabled globally and locally through blockchain trading platforms. Using blockchain technology will also give them the means of investing in companies and their specific activities without having minimums or going through intermediaries that take a percentage of the investment.

Decentralized autonomous organizations (DAOs) are already out there and making DAO investment pools happen for a few risk-tolerant and more technically savvy investors. It may be some time before an institutional investor utilizes one or a portfolio manager recommends putting money into a DAO-based vehicle for her clients.

DAOs remove a lot of the necessary paperwork and bureaucracy involved in investing by creating a blockchain-based voting system and giving shares to those who invest in their product. To any blockchain, the "code as law" concept makes it unforgiving. The risks are many, particularly when there is poorly written code that executes in unintended ways. The consequences are that hacks to this system can be severe. The transparent nature of the original system, the poor code, gives hackers a wider attack vector and allows them to attack multiple times as they gain more and more information each time.

In the following section, I discuss the effects and benefits of blockchain technology on the world economy.

Border-free payroll

Our world is global, and companies don't have borders. Instant and nearly free payroll is enticing and would save a lot of headaches for organizations. But there are drawbacks, too.

The largest risks will be with the loss of funds through hacking. If you're compensated in cryptocurrency, and you were hacked, it would be impossible to retrieve your funds. There's no dispute resolution center. There's no customer service to complain to for the loss of these funds. Thieves of digital currency have global access while being somewhat anonymous. The hacker could be anywhere.

With the current structure of blockchains, the consumer is responsible for his own security. Currently, customers don't have the main burden of protecting and insuring themselves from a loss. Larger companies and governments offer protection and insurance, and they have for as long as anyone can remember. Regular individuals haven't had to protect themselves in this manner since they stopped holding their own gold during medieval times (more or less).

These challenges haven't spotted companies from processing payroll using cryptocurrency. Bitwage and BitPay are both competing in the market for payroll processing via Bitcoin. Bitwage allows employees and independent contractors to receive part of their paychecks in cryptocurrency, even if their employers don't offer the option. BitPay, on the other hand, has payroll service providers Zuman and Incoin integrated into its payment and payroll APIs. Again, early adoption is happening in areas that had nonexistent or inadequate solutions before.

Faster and better trade

Blockchains will facilitate faster and possible more inclusive trade. Global trade finance has restricted in recent years. Some banks like Barclays have even pulled out of growing African markets. They leave behind a vacuum for financing trade. Companies still need capital to ship their goods.

DAOs and micro investments could meet that need and give investors more profitable returns than are currently available on the market. Transparency of all the goods being sold, secure identity, and seamless global tracking that is all connected to a blockchain would open up this opportunity for small investors.

The interoperability between currencies, which companies like Ripple facilitate, will also allow for more trade because they offer flexible ways of calculating foreign exchange rates than through the transfer mechanisms. The introduction of more popular digital currencies into foreign currency exchanges will add to the adaptability and integration of underserved markets.

BitPesa is a company that converts M-pesa phone minutes from Kenya into Bitcoin. With this technology, it offers businesses a faster and cheaper way to send or receive payments between Africa and China. The trade between Africa and China is a market of over $170 billion. It takes days to settle payments across borders, and the fees are high. When you use BitPesa's digital platform, payments are instantaneous and cheap.

Guaranteed payments

Guaranteed payments that are permitted through blockchain-backed transactions will increase trade in places where trust is low. Poorer countries can compete on the same playing field as wealthier nations within these types of systems. As this happens over the next ten years, the global economies will shift. The cost of commodities and labor may increase.

Global companies pay their employees based on competitive pricing, as well as on employees' previous salaries. If blockchains allow for equality across economic divides, it won't happen overnight. Developers and other knowledge workers would be the exception because it'll be easier for them to support themselves based on anonymous work.

Financial inclusion and equal global trade are very important topics for governments. Adoption of digital currencies will more likely be done nationwide in small and developing countries. Most large countries have decentralized power structures that prevent quick changes to vital systems like money.

Their central power structures of small countries will allow them to leapfrog over legacy infrastructure and bureaucracy. For example, most African and South American countries don't have landlines or addresses, but they all have smartphones and ability to create cryptocurrency wallets. The missing piece is overall trade liquidity and capacity to pay for basic needs such as utilities, rent, and food through a cryptocurrency.

Micropayments: The new nature of transactions

Micropayments are the new form of transactions. Credit card companies may use blockchain technology to settle the transaction, reduce fraud, and lower their own costs.

Global institutions like Visa and MasterCard, which provide the benefit of delayed payment, will always be needed by consumers in capitalistic societies. Even if the backend changes, you still have the same access points for customers. But physical cards will go away. In fact, that's happening now, even without blockchain technology. With blockchain technology, the customer identities behind payments will be more hardened against theft.

People still need credit to operate a business and get by personally. Credit card companies will keep making money through transaction fees. Credits run the world, and capital markets will always exist in our current social structure. The cost of sending money between groups will decrease, but that's a good thing for financial institutions. They want to focus on the service of providing their customers with the best choices in their investment or banking markets.

Squeezing Out Fraud

Bitcoin was created as an answer to the financial crisis, where fraud and other unethical actions caused the world economy to collapse. It shifts from a "trust or doesn't trust" view of the world to a trustless system. This subtle difference is lost to most. A *trustless system* is one in which you equally trust and mistrust every person within the network. More important, the blockchain provides a framework that allows transactions to occur without trust.

These same types of frameworks can be used in more than just exchanging value over the network. Let me share an example that will help illustrate the potential.

I go to a bar and the man at the door stops me and asks to see my ID. I reach into my wallet and hand him my driver's license. My license has a lot of information on it that the bouncer doesn't need, nor should he have access to (like my address). All he needs from the ID is that I'm over the age of 21. He doesn't even need to know how old I am — just that I meet the regulation requirements.

In the future, blockchain ID systems will let you choose what information you expose to what person and at what level. The more anonymous data it has, the safer it will be. Blockchain systems will help curb the theft of identity and data by not sharing information with those who don't need it or have permission to see it.

Another aspect of blockchain technology is that it will shift fraud from where it happened (past tense) to where it is currently happening in real time. Within our current system, audits are fractional post-mortems of what has happened. A group of outside auditors comes, pulls a few random files, and sees if everything is in place. Doing anything beyond this is too costly and time-consuming.

Record systems that have blockchain technology integrated within them will be able to audit a file as it's created, flagging incomplete or unusual files as they're created. This will give managers the tools they need to proactively correct files before they become a problem.

Another feature of blockchain systems will be the ability to share the data with third parties transparently. In the future, sharing data will be as easy as emailing a zip file, except the receiver will then have access to the original copy, not a copy if the file sent across email. When someone sends a file, he has a version on his computer and the receiver has a version. With blockchain technology, the two people will only be sharing one version.

Blockchains act as a third party that witnesses the age and creation of files. They can tell at a granular level each person who interacted with a file across systems, internally and externally. They can show what is missing from a file, not just the data that is contained in it now. Blockchain files can also be shared in a redacted fashion that does not compromise the validity of documents.

What this means is that you'll be able to see the age of a file, the complete history of a file, and what it looked like over time as it evolved. More interestingly, you'll also be able to see if anything is missing from a file. This concept is called *proving the negative*. Most file systems at this point can only tell you what they have within them. But you'll be able to tell what a file *doesn't* have.

Auditing will be less expensive and more complete. Updating audit rules could be done in a more centralized way. When regulatory nodes within a blockchain network have a shared and transparent view into asset transactions, the reporting of these transactions can be done through the regulator's location, without mandating 100 or more other institutions to adhere to the same rule set.

Blockchain-based systems that are fully integrated across an organization will be able to know where every penny was spent. The last mile of how money is spent is the most difficult to account for across organizations and governments. Because it's so difficult to account for, those wishing to steal funds have the opening they need.

The last mile could become a company's greatest opportunity to save wasted resources and identify corrupt individuals. Nonprofits that have strict guidelines on accounting for how they spend their money could benefit from this type of system the most. They could meet their needs for auditing and accountability to their donors without impeding them in their greater missions for good.

One system that has been explored would integrate directly into the workflow of aid workers. This system was originally designed to track medical records but could also track back all the supplies that are used with each medical patient. The benefits of this system would be monumental, given that so much fraud and theft occurs within the NGO world.

Chapter **13**

Real Estate

Real estate will be one of the industries most impacted by innovations in blockchain technology. The impact will be felt in every country in a slightly different way. In the western world, we might see the advent of things like transparent mortgage-backed securities traded on blockchain-enabled exchanges. In China, blockchain integration is already happening with things like notarization, an essential component of real estate transactions. In the developing world, blockchains hold the most promise because they may be able to free capital and increase trade.

This chapter dives into the innovations that are already happening around the world in the real estate industry. I also fill you in on possible changes coming down the road and the significant implications of blockchain technology.

Real estate holds much of the world's wealth and economic stability. The industry will be changing very quickly over the next few years, and knowing where these changes will occur and how you and your company can take advantage of them will be a benefit.

Eliminating Title Insurance

Title insurance is compensation for financial loss from defects in your title for a real estate purchase. It's required if you take out a mortgage on your home or if you refinance it. Title insurance protects the bank's investment against title problems that might not be found in the public records, are missed in the title search, or occur from fraud or forgery.

Title insurance is necessary in places that use common law to govern their title systems. The buyer is responsible for ensuring that the seller's title is good. Within these systems, a title search is done and insurance is bought. In areas that use a Torrens title system a buyer can rely on the information in the land register and doesn't need to look beyond those records.

Blockchain technology has been proposed as a supplement to help consumers in common law title systems. The idea is simple: Blockchains are fantastic public recordkeeping systems; they also can't be backdated or changed without a record. In theory, blockchains could transform common law systems into distributed Torrens title systems.

First, though, many challenges must be overcome. Each county in a common law system has its own land records office, where all the deeds or records that transfer title to any piece of land or any interest in any land in the county are recorded and noted. The United States alone has thousands of counties. The thousands of individual offices create silos of data. Blockchain doesn't change the law or how the records are organized.

New laws would need to be created that dictate that all interest and transfer of land must be recorded within a single system to be valid. Then it's just a Torrens system and may make blockchain technology redundant. The exception would be in areas where there is a lot of fraud within the land registry.

In the following sections, I dig into the real estate industry and where blockchains add value.

Protected industries

Every industry has self-protecting systems to keep new competition out. It might be a high regulatory burden, government-granted monopolies, or high startup costs. The industry that has built up around the buying and selling of real estate hasn't changed much in the last 40 years and is ripe for disruption. Many different parties contribute to the process.

Here are the different industries that are built around the buying and selling of homes:

>> **Real estate agents:** A real estate agent helps you compare different neighborhoods and find a home. He often helps you negotiate a price and

communicates with the seller on your behalf. This service is valuable, and it's not likely to be displaced by blockchain technology. You can already buy a home without a real estate agent — people choose to work with them because they improve the process.

» **Home inspectors:** Home inspectors uncover defects with the house before you buy it — defects that could cost you money down the road. The defects home inspectors find can be used to negotiate with the seller for a better price. In the future, homes will continue to have wear and tear — that'll never change. But blockchain technology could be used to record repairs to property and defects found in the inspection.

» **Closing representatives:** At closing, the final step is settlement. The closing representative supervises and coordinates the closing documents, records them, and releases the money to the appropriate parties. Closing representatives may be displaced by blockchain technology — the functions performed by closing representatives could be built into smart contracts or chaincode.

» **Mortgage lenders and servicers:** Mortgage lenders and servicers provide funds for a mortgage and collect the ongoing mortgage payments. They won't be displaced with blockchain software, but they may use blockchain technology to help them reduce costs with recordkeeping and auditing.

» **Real estate appraisers:** The real estate appraiser's job is to look at a property and determine how much it's worth. The appraisal process is done every time a property is bought or refinanced. Companies like Zillow have taken a lot of the legwork out of knowing the market value, but each home is unique and needs to be assessed periodically. Even in the real estate mortgage process, multiple appeals may be called for to meet everyone's needs. It might be useful to record this data within a blockchain as a public witness.

» **Loan officers:** Loan officers use your credit, financial, and employment information to see if you qualify for a mortgage. They then match what you're eligible for with products that they sell. Like a real estate agent, a loan officer helps you get the best option across a spectrum of choices. Blockchain software may be used to help loan officers keep track of documents that they give you and audit the process for fair lending law compliance.

» **Loan processors:** A loan processor assists loan officers in preparing mortgage loan information and the application for presentation to the underwriter. Software that pulls the buyer's source information is being explored. It's not blockchain technology, but it could be disruptive for this position.

» **Mortgage underwriters:** A mortgage underwriter determines whether you're eligible for a mortgage loan. She approves or rejects your mortgage loan application based on your credit history, employment, assets, and debts. Organizations are exploring automating the underwriting process using artificial intelligence. It's not blockchain technology, though.

Each of these agents serves a core purpose that helps protect the buyer, seller, and mortgage provider. In most industries, the cost of doing business goes down over time — improvements in efficiency brought about by competition and innovation contribute to driving down cost. The mortgage industry is attractive as a candidate for blockchain innovation, because the opposite has occurred: The cost of business has gone up. The typical U.S. mortgage is over 500 pages and costs $7,500 to originate. This is three times what it cost ten years ago. Blockchain technology can meet the needs of protecting the buyer, seller, and mortgage provider while reducing the cost to do so.

Consumers and Fannie Mae

The Federal National Mortgage Association (known as Fannie Mae) is both a government-sponsored enterprise and a publicly traded company. It's currently the leading source of financing for mortgage lenders and has dominated the market post-recession as private money left.

Since the recession, 95 percent of all home loans made in the United States have come through Fannie Mae. This is about $5 trillion in mortgage assets. With few exceptions, loans that are not done through Fannie Mae or its close cousin, Freddie Mac, are jumbo loans (typically more than $417,000 each). These loans are still funded through private money.

Fannie Mae has an automated program used by loan originators to qualify a borrower. It helps them navigate guidelines for a conventional loan. Lenders run your loan application through Fannie Mae's computer system, and it spits out an answer of either approve or decline for your loan. Online platforms are using this new software to reach consumers, allowing them to bypass traditional retail locations. Fannie Mae and Freddie Mac are exploring blockchain technology to even further streamline this process and reach customers directly.

Mortgages in the Blockchain World

A mortgage in a blockchain world won't seem that much different than a mortgage in the traditional world. The part that you'll notice is that a blockchain mortgage will be less expensive at closing.

Given that most people only ever buy a few homes in their lifetimes, the difference may not seem like a big deal. But the money does add up. Blockchain technology could lower the cost to originate a mortgage back to pre-2007 levels.

Reducing your origination costs

Mortgage origination costs have increased, and the reason is simple: Banks fear fines that they can incur if they mess up any part of the mortgage process. So, the industry has put in steps to help make sure that they meet all the requirements at the time of origination and years later when they're audited. Big banks have paid billions in fines from the mishandling of documents. They're now required not only to have all the essential documents, but also to prove that they followed the correct process and sent you all the necessary documents.

Blockchain-based products reduce the redundancy that banks began incorporating into their process after the recession. Recordkeeping and auditing expenses have skyrocketed since the introduction of the Dodd–Frank Wall Street Reform and Consumer Protection Act, and blockchain technology could reduce that cost.

Companies wanting to meet the needs of banks with a blockchain solution would need to let banks prove that they followed the guidelines set out in Dodd–Frank. It would also help banks document why they made certain decisions on loans, and help them locate documents that were used in origination, even if they aren't in possession of them.

Blockchain applications could put close to $4,000 back on the table for the average home purchase. The mortgage industry is a lot like the car loan industry and the credit card industry. Similar applications could reduce the administration cost that these industries have due to consumer protection laws, while at the same time letting companies meet those requirements.

Knowing your last-known document

One of the largest cost drivers in the mortgage origination process often comes years after the loan was first made. Sometimes those facilitating the loan process add unneeded documents into client files, or old files that aren't used to originate a loan are left in the folder. Also, duplicate records may occur. When it comes time to audit the file, there is too much information to sift through. Banks pay money to outside firms to check their records and try to determine what documents were used in the final dissection on your loan.

Blockchain software can solve this problem in an elegant way. Blockchains are distributed recordkeeping systems that allow for multiple parties to collaborate on data over time without losing track of what that data looked like at any given point along the way. This means that the half dozen individual organizations that collaborate to help you buy your home can now all interact on the same chain.

A chain in this use case would start with you. Your chain would then have subchains added to it over time, such as the purchase of a home. You could then authorize others — such as banks, employers, credit agencies, appraisal companies, and the like — to write against the chain. They would each add their data to your chain, and the other authorized parties could read this data and add their own.

Blockchains would change the need for central repositories for files. It would automate some of the processing of the paperwork, and would always give a clear history of your loan, reducing the need to audit and prepare documents to be verified.

This is a big idea, but it doesn't require the whole ecosystem to collaborate. Each branch that does would strengthen the system and add value, much like the way each addition person who owned a fax machine made the power of having one that much more useful.

Forecasting Regional Trends

Blockchain has been fighting an uphill battle to become a mainstream software solution. It is often met with fear because many people don't understand how it works or what the actual implications are for its widespread implementation. Also, many of the early advocates, like early adopters of any new technology, were seen as a little "out there." Blockchain gets caught up in the bad PR of Bitcoin and illicit and illegal things being done with the technology.

However, 2016 was a turning point for the industry. It became clear that block-chain would be disruptive and that those who wanted to be on the positive side of that equation had to come up with a blockchain strategy.

Every major bank began programs to investigate and experiment with blockchain or joined a consortium. Many moved first to interbank settlement and cross-border transfers, which are relatively straightforward applications for blockchains. The next and more transformative evolutions will be the systems and data that are secured through decentralization.

In the following sections, I cover the trends in blockchain technology in the United States, Europe, China, and Africa.

The United States and Europe: Infrastructure congestion

The United States and European countries may take longer to implement blockchain technology than other countries. Even though companies in these countries spend billions of dollars on infrastructure maintenance, it's just that: maintenance. There are already existing solutions to the problems that blockchains want to solve. It's not just a matter of saying that blockchains would offer a better solution — that solution must be ten times better than an existing system or be able to implement through integration.

One of the main challenges that the United States faces is that it's decentralized in the distribution of power and decision-making. Each county and each state will come up with its own rules for how to implement or use blockchain technology. This process has already begun.

Blockchains can trigger money transmitter laws and regulations. In the United States, it's clearer at a federal level what types of businesses are considered money transmitters. Given that all the essential public blockchains currently use a cryptocurrency token to drive security, the issue is clouded, which has given rise to private and permission blockchains that operate without tokens.

State licensure requirements are ambiguous for companies using blockchain technology for applications other than payments. Regulations and laws will be enacted to protect consumers. Europe already has laws around "being forgotten." Compliance with these rules could be tricky when data entered into blockchains is around forever and can't be removed by anyone, even if they wanted to.

Being engaged in money transmission in many U.S. states is a felony. The hard consequences of overstepping law through innovation compel blockchain companies to spend significantly more money and time on compliance — to the tune of an average of $2 million to $5 million per year per company. The legal fees are heavy burdens for these technology startups.

The legislation of each state as applied to the blockchain industry are not clear yet. New York and Vermont have begun integrating this technology into law. New York has increased the cost to be in compliance and driven innovation to move to friendlier locations. Vermont, on the other hand, passed a law that makes blockchain records admissible in court.

Luxembourg created a legal framework for electronic payment establishments in 2011 and was early on the idea of "electronic money." Luxembourg and the UK have become home to many blockchain companies because the regulatory environment is easier for them to navigate and afford. For less than $1 million, blockchain businesses can obtain a payment instrument license in the European Union. This license grants companies access to 28 EU countries. This approach has allowed the EU to advance beyond the United States in fintech innovation.

China: First out of the gate

China realized that citizens were using it to move value out of the country undetected and were generating new wealth in a less captive system. Because of this, China has revised its regulations on cryptocurrency several times, which has had a significant impact on the market price of Bitcoins.

Industries inside of China are looking to blockchains to solve many of the same problems seen in other parts of the world. They've been quick to use blockchains to supplement what they've already been doing, adding layers of certainty to things like Internet of Things (IoT) and notarization. Whereas Western countries have a more distributed and decentralized power structure, China has a more centralized one. This allows China to move quickly to both regulate and innovate.

China Ledger, a blockchain coalition with support from the Chinese National Assembly, the ruling body of China, is a good example of swift action by both regulatory bodies and industry. China Ledger has attracted Anthony Di Iorio and Vitalik Buterin, both Ethereum founders. It also has support from Bitcoin core developer Jeff Garzik and UBS Innovation Manager Alex Baltin.

The developing world: Roadblocks to blockchain

The future is here — it's just not distributed. This is especially true in developing countries, which often have a greater need for technology, yet don't have the same resources or the right political environment to allow those innovations to take root. Some small countries try protectionist measures that block the importation of goods that could be made within their borders; other countries mistrust the quality and benevolence of products and services that come from the outsides sources as well. On a darker note, some political systems benefit too greatly from the inefficiencies and ambiguities that their legal system has in place to change.

Hernando de Soto Polar is a Peruvian economist and author who has spoken widely on an informal economy and the importance of business and property rights. One of the prominent issues that keeps the developing world undeveloped is *dead capital*. The property which is informally held and not legally recognized or the current systems in place cannot be trusted. For owners of this land, it is difficult or impossible to finance and sell. The uncertainty also decreases the value of the assets. The western world has been able to borrow against assets and sell them relatively freely. This has driven innovation and economic prosperity.

The technology that is enabled by blockchains could change that reality for developing countries very quickly. Clear ownership records for land would mean that it would be sellable and financeable. This would make the beachfront property of Colombia irresistible. Irreversible payments and true known identity would open credit and commerce in new ways.

Many startups and hackers have come together to try to make this future vision a reality. Even larger global players like the World Bank have had repeated meeting about blockchain and its impact in the developing world. Bitcoin and blockchain are making inroads in Africa where local currencies and infrastructure are deeply mistrusted. BitPesa, a payment and trading platform servicing many countries in Africa, has begun expanding to the UK and Europe. It has also started widening its service offerings to things like payroll.

As many roadblocks as developing countries have toward development and innovation, they also have advantages that western countries will never overcome. The lack of existing infrastructure in developing countries makes it easier for them to leapfrog Western nations. This was evident in the proliferation of cellphones in developing countries. Developing countries also don't have the same regulatory bodies and consumer protections. This is particularly attractive for blockchain startups that fall into the gray zone in western countries. Developing countries often have fewer decision makers, making it easier to meet people who have the power to change.

Chapter **14**

Insurance

B lockchain insurance technology is situated to change how individuals and companies buy and obtain insurance coverage, and it's coming faster than you might think! You need to understand the implications of these new technologies that are just now on the horizon.

In this chapter, I explain how these new technologies work and their core limitations. I show you how Internet of Things (IoT) devices will collaborate with insurance providers. I also describe how self-executing blockchain contracts will shape policies and company structures.

This chapter prepares you for the fundamental changes in technology that may shift the burden of proof. After reading this chapter, you'll be able to make more educated decisions about blockchain-based insurance coverage and payments. You'll understand how the cost of coverage will affect you and the different types of coverage that will become available to you in the future.

Precisely Tailoring Coverage

IoT devices, immutable data, decentralized autonomous organizations (DAOs), and smart contracts are all shifting the development of insurance for consumers. The convergence of all these technologies is possible because of the development of blockchains.

Blockchains do a few things really well that will allow for two major shifts in how insurance will be bought and sold in the future: Individuals will be able to gain more custom coverage, and new markets will open up that weren't possible before due to costs.

Insuring the individual

Insurance built around the individual will allow for a significant shift of priorities. Asset management will be less critical, and the insurers will be able to focus on risk calculation and matching supply and demand.

You could create a marketplace platform that insures customers. There are many ways that you could organize this new business. One possibility would be an on-demand marketplace where users post their requests, either standardized by custom smart contract or by Chaincode contract. If you haven't read about these types of new self-executing digital contracts, check out Chapter 5 on Ethereum and Chapter 9 on Hyperledger.

With this type of model, you, as the insurer, could calculate the premium for the specific demand, based on historical data and other risk calculation factors in your risk model. If the customer is satisfied with the offer, the customer can bid or subscribe, depending on the demand model being utilized.

This new type of insurance could be adopted by peer-to-peer (P2P) or crowd-funded insurance or a traditional insurance company that adopts the technology. Either way, both are created in a decentralized cryptocurrency ledger with the use of smart contracts/Chaincode, which guarantee the payment from the customer to the investor and vice versa if an incident occurs. Blockchain is key here, because it enables a few things that weren't feasible or secure a few years ago.

Blockchains create near frictionless transfer of value meaning micropayments are feasible because the transaction fees are so low. You can now open up new markets that did not have a working monetary system or legal system or instances where the cost of transactions and disputes outweighed the benefit of offering coverage.

You can use DAOs, with smart contracts, to govern large groups at a fraction of the cost and time. You could use this model to incorporate and administer your new company, and possibly crowd-fund insurance platforms.

The self-executing nature of smart contracts could also illuminate many of the cost of claims adjustment and third parties that help with the processing and collection of funds.

The legality of all this is still in question. Determining privacy concerns and consumer rights is difficult. The country also has its own regulations and disclosures. However, when those regulations are met, the insurance industry and the consumer's experience with insurance will shift substantially.

The new world of micro insurance

Micro insurance is insurance to protect low-income people against risk, such as accident, illness, and natural disaster. It has become more feasible through blockchain technology.

When thinking about micro insurance, pay attention to two categories (which can go hand in hand):

>> Insurance targeted to low-income households, farmers, and other entities where the insurance is designed around specific needs — typically, a low-premium and index-based insurance

>> Insurance that deals with low-value products or services

The biggest issue with these types of contracts within traditional insurance models is that their handling costs are disproportionately high and make it unattractive to serve these markets.

The low-friction attribute of blockchains allows them to move value at extremely low cost, nearly instantly anywhere in the world, with no charge backs, opens up the opportunity of serving more people and at lower costs.

The key advantage of blockchain is that the creation of smart contracts allows for secure transactions without any middleman, so insurance has significantly lower costs.

The blockchain micro insurance principle is simple and consists of four steps:

1. Lending/insuring agreement proposal

A person can offer to lend his property through his insurance provider, if the property is digitally registered. The offer can be sent to the potential user, either through the insurance company channels or via a public platform such as Facebook.

2. Agreement review

The borrower can then review the proposal that he received and accept or decline it. The offer is kept in the public records, and if the borrower accepts the proposal, he can purchase the insurance through standard payment channels, and the process moves to the third step.

3. Agreement signature and notarization

If both parties are on the same page, the insurance is paid for and the borrower receives the property in question, the agreement is digitally signed and notarized onto a blockchain. This makes it virtually tamper-proof. All the transaction information is safely stored with a clear audit trail if it's ever needed.

4. Confirmation tokens

Both parties receive special digital tokens that serve as the proof of identity for the agreement in question. These tokens are used to cryptologically confirm that both parties have signed the agreement.

Besides this ease of use, smart contracts allow for index-based insurance, which is very useful for agricultural insurance and other fields where the values depend greatly on dynamic factors that can be accurately documented by trusted third parties. In this particular case, insured farmers can receive automated payouts when particular conditions, such as drought, are reported by verified meteorological databases, thus further reducing potential service cost.

Witnessing for You: The Internet of Things

Blockchains enable the creation of a new type of identity for both people and things. They build on a traditional model where a certificate authority issues a certificate. For people, that certificate would be a document such as a birth certificate or a driver's license. But "things" have similar certificates that help consumers validate quality and authenticity.

These types of certificates have been knocked off for years. More and more sophisticated security has gone into their creation, but this increases the cost. Blockchains allow for the recording of these traditional certificates in an unalterable history that anyone can look up and reference. An added feature is the ability to update those records as new events occur.

IoT devices can now publish all kinds of data autonomously to their records and update the current state they're in. Now that IoT devices can speak for themselves and have their histories and identities published and sharable with third parties, insurance will be just one of the many industries affected.

IoT projects in insurance

IoT will likely have significant impact in three areas of your life: the connected car, the connected home, and the connected self.

The IoT is, at its core, a disruptive technology and, as such, it'll change the shape of a broad range of industries, such as automotive original equipment manufacturers (OEMs), home security, and cable and mobile providers. In that mix are insurance companies — in particular, the ones that work with property and casualty (P&C) policies.

The data gathered by the sensors in the new appliances and devices, along with the automation and additional control options, will lead to new possibilities when it comes to new companies emerging in the insurance industry. Combined with the blockchain decentralized ledgers and smart contracts, the whole process could be automated to a level that would've been impossible before.

WARNING

The new, always online, lifestyle that comes with such a radical shift in technology removes some of the existing risks, but it introduces new ones, the most important of which is information security. All this means that the risk factors will have to be recalculated. For example, self-driving cars will have reduced risk of accident due to the absence of human error, but the reliability of the technology will be in question until we have enough data from real-world application.

Implications of actionable big data

Big data has been a thing since 2000, and nowadays it's a $200 billion industry and of particular importance to the financial sector. However, big data comes with a number of problems that only grow with its presence in the everyday world:

>> **Control:** If you have a big multinational enterprise or a consortium, the issue of data sharing becomes fairly significant. Version control is imperfect, and it can sometimes be really difficult to tell which is the latest, most up-to-date copy.

>> **Data trustworthiness:** How do you prove if you're the creator of said data, or someone else is? What happens with corrupted data?

>> **Data monetization and transfer:** How can you transfer, buy, or sell rights to any data, and be sure that it's the only copy there is?

>> **Data changing:** How do you ensure that data is not being changed when it's not supposed to?

All these problems are solvable using cryptocurrency and blockchain. The large challenge that the industry is working through now is scaling blockchain technology to accommodate the cost and data storage demands of enterprises.

Taking Out the Third Party in Insurance

One of the greatest advantages that blockchain tech introduces into the modern finance world is the smart contracts that allow for business transactions without the involvement of a third party, such as banks or intermediaries.

Put simply, a *smart contract* is a protocol that allows for two parties to record their transaction into a blockchain. These contracts can be used for pretty much anything, from exchange of physical goods (that have digital signatures) to exchange of information or money.

The key security feature here is that, unlike the ordinary financial database, the information is distributed to and verified by all the computers in the network, making it decentralized. The data is unique and not able to be copied; the audit trail is immutable.

Decentralized security

At the core of current business models is something that could be called the *centralized trust paradigm,* in which middlemen such as bankers, brokers, and lawyers coordinate and ensure the veracity of financial transactions and exchanges of goods.

Centralization comes with certain inherent security risks, such as data corruption and theft. Blockchains combat this by creating a decentralized system that is based on mutual distrust of all the participants that keep each other in check.

In order to create such a system, you create a distributed ledger that uses cryptocurrency (like Bitcoin, Ethereum, or Factom), where each participant is both the user of the system and responsible for its maintenance and upkeep.

Crowdfunded coverage

Similar to standard crowdfunding initiatives, the idea is to pool resources from numerous entities or persons in order to cover for an unexpected shortcoming in an insurance plan. For example, a retirement insurance plan could kick in only at the age of 65, but a person could be forced to retire early because of unforeseen circumstances, and additional funds would be needed by the unfortunate individual.

Economic disparity has grown over the years, and numerous underinsured or uninsured people could benefit from such a system. Crowdfunding can potentially provide benefits to all three parties in question:

>> **Insurers** gain increased revenue because more people are interested in their plans. They gain access to a greater portion of the underinsured population. In addition, the insuring company could improve its brand recognition — it could be seen as a company that cares.

>> **Donors** could benefit from possible tax exemptions, if the structure of the campaign allows it, or they could gain other benefits, such as discounts or free services.

>> **Seekers** (those looking for insurance) obviously stand to gain the most, as they can get better protection and more affordable coverage.

Cognizant proposed interesting insights to crowdfunding insurance in its white-paper. You can find it at https://goo.gl/u3Kd3U.

The implications of DAO insurance

DAOs are corporate entities that have no full-time employees, but are able to per-form all the functions that a standard corporation can. The ability to create such an entity stems directly from the improvement in blockchain algorithms, which has happened over the last few years and has created what is commonly known as blockchain 2.0.

A DAO is, in essence, a form of an advanced smart contract. The DAO is able treat DAO as a corporation where all its individual policy users are shareholders, while the corporation itself never is in direct control of any particular group or individual.

In the same manner, a DAO is never under control of the developers, and they don't issue or deny policies. It's strictly a peer-to-peer insurance model. Although vulnerabilities regarding identity verification still exist, this system will be improved, and in reality, the same issues exist even in the current, centralized insurance systems.

Chapter **15**

Government

n this chapter, I introduce you to the exciting innovations that are taking place inside governments and the companies that support them with innovative blockchain projects.

Everyday business is affected by scams and fraud, and this chapter explains how governments are fighting back against cybercrime and identity theft. You also find out about smart cities initiatives, which will be critical to economic growth and sustainability — many are using blockchain technology to bridge technological gaps.

The Smart Cities of Asia

Smart cities are taking advantage of modern technology to enhance infrastructure function, and safety, and improve things like traffic and air quality. The business of becoming a smart city is booming, and almost every larger municipality has embraced the smart city concept.

Blockchain is especially useful when integrated with the Internet of Things (IoT) used by smart cities. Several interesting projects are being piloted now for commercial deployment. The U.S. Department of Homeland Security is exploring securing IoT devices used by Customs and Border Protection (CBP). Companies such as Slock.it are allowing connected objects to use the blockchain to enter into smart contracts; its first product was a blockchain-enabled smart lock, which could be used be Airbnb customers. The integration of these technologies allows devices to use their sensors to set up smart contracts. This same technology could be used by city parking meters.

Figure 15-1 shows the home page of Singapore's Smart Nation project. Singapore has been courting startups from around the world to develop new technology in its "regulatory sandbox." It's a welcome invitation to blockchain technology companies that have been operating in the *gray zone* (where there is not a clear regulatory framework established), however many countries, like Singapore are taking direct action to define the space and let companies know what is allowed and not allowed.

FIGURE 15-1:
Singapore's Smart Nation project.

Blockchain technology could also be used to share information between networks in a smart city securely. Many cities are exploring how to use blockchain to alleviate traffic jams. Singapore's Smart Nation project hopes to use the mobile phones of its citizens to measure the conditions of their bus rides, and then analyze the data to see when roads need to be upgraded. Singapore has been a leader in smart city development and has begun developing smart cities in other countries.

In this section, I walk you through some of the many blockchain efforts that are taking place in Asia.

Singapore satellite cities in India

The Indian government launched its Smart Cities Mission in 2015, with the intention of building 100 new smart cities. Many of these developments will be in the Delhi Mumbai Industrial Corridor, which is a 620-mile (1,000km) stretch between Delhi and Mumbai. Infrastructure worth $11 billion has already been planned across 33 cities, and much of the development will be funded through a public–private model. The project is expected to attract $90 billion in foreign investment, which will be used to create business parks, manufacturing zones and smart cities, all of which will be situated along a delegated rail freight corridor.

These smart cities are being developed as India's economy industrializes and the population becomes more urbanized. State intervention in the form of centrally planned cities is necessary in order to prevent the existing cities from becoming overcrowded and unlivable. India is particularly vulnerable to climate change because of its immense and impoverished population. Because of this, it's important that these cities are sustainable and smart. They need low-energy housing materials, intelligent grids, planned transportation, integrated IT systems, e-governance, and innovative water harvesting.

Singapore is a prime example of an intelligently planned city. Despite the high population density, it has excellent infrastructure and a high quality of life. Many of Singapore's private organizations have the knowledge and resources that are needed to develop India's smart cities. In collaboration with the Indian government, the private sector would be able to provide the capital, skills, and technology that are necessary for such large plans.

Andhara Pradesh and the Monetary Authority of Singapore have announced a financial technology (fintech) innovation partnership, with a primary focus on blockchain and digital payments. Singapore aims to develop a marketplace for fintech solutions in India.

Singaporean leadership has shown interest in partnering with India to develop a smart city as well as a new capital for Andhra Pradesh, a state in the southeast. It's setting up committees to analyze the potential for collaboration in India's plan to build 100 new cities, as well as further developing the infrastructure across 500 existing towns and cities.

India's minister of urban development has been in talks with both Singapore's current prime minister and its former prime minister. He has been seeking Singapore's expertise in smart cities, particularly focusing on intelligent transport systems, enhanced water management, and e-governance. The minister of urban development has also been examining Singapore's public housing schemes, as well as their private housing regulations. Funding structures for transport infrastructure have been looked at as well.

Indian authorities have also engaged a team of Singaporean experts to assist the development of a satellite town in Himachal Pradesh. The 49-acre (20-hectare) project aims to help decongest Shimla, a town that has had a massive population rise in the past few decades. The Singaporeans will assist in educational, residential, and commercial aspects of the town under development.

Both Singapore and Malaysia have shown interest in investing in another satellite town near Jathia Devi. The Singaporean government is undertaking a study that will assess various options. The state government of Himachal Pradesh is looking at developing five satellite towns near existing cities, using a private–public funding model.

Singapore's Ascendas-Singbridge launched its eighth IT park in India. The 59-acre (24-hectare) International Tech Park Gurgaon is expected to have its first building completed in the middle of the year. The $400 million project aims to offer 8 million square feet of business space to help accommodate India's burgeoning IT sector.

China's big data problem

Blockchain technology is widely being discussed in China as a way to enhance the reliability of big data. People are looking at it as a way to solve the trust issue involved in sharing data between two or more parties that don't have aligned incentives. Blockchain technology offers many new solutions to track ownership, origin, and authenticity.

Peernova is a promising U.S. company that is tackling big data problems. It previously focused on Bitcoin mining but pivoted into the blockchain space and raised $4 million from Zhejiang Zhongnan Holdings Groups, a construction company from China. Peernova plans to use blockchain technology to query traditional databases and track changes.

The use cases are to verify any changes to subsets of large data stores and use the more efficient and complete cryptographic audits instead of a traditional auditor to provide a reference point for a company. It hopes to help hedge funds calculate the tax liability of their investments by using blockchain to trace the history of money that has been invested over the years.

Dalian Wanda, the biggest real estate developer in China, is also getting into the blockchain game. It has teamed up with big data software company Cloudera to launch a blockchain project called Hercules. It sees the potential to use blockchain technology to make predictions derived from big data actionable for managers as they're occurring, moving managers from reactive to proactive in situations like modifications to their protocols, as well as monitor user behavior within their systems.

Dalian Wanda and Cloudera aim to keep developing Hercules and integrate their technology into a variety of industries that rely on IT and big data. Project Hercules will act as an open-source suite that supports the needs of businesses. It makes it easier for organizations to deploy and manage blockchain apps on large data clusters.

You might find it odd to see a digital mining company partner with a traditional construction company to tackle auditing issues for hedge funds, or real estate companies working with big data to solve issues for system administrators, but this is the wild west of the blockchain world. The shortage in blockchain talent and the high demand for blockchain projects and investment are fueling this environment.

The Battle for the Financial Capital of the World

Blockchain technology has come into its own since breaking into the public consciousness with a plethora of news coverage in 2015. Many startups have been working on beta and pre-launch builds since then, with nearly 2,000 new blockchain startups forming overnight in 2016. Many of these will finally go to market sometime in 2017 and 2018 in Singapore, Dubai, and London where the regulatory bodies welcome innovation and compete to be the financial mecca of the world. This isn't just about fintech and smart cities for these leaders. It's a race for relevance in a world shifting to borderless and financially fluid global citizens.

London's early foresight

In 2016, the central government of the United Kingdom put out a report called "Distributed Ledger Technology: Beyond Block Chain" (https://goo.gl/asIz6L), which asserted that distributed ledger technology (blockchains) could be used to reduce corruption, errors, and fraud, and make various processes more efficient. They also stated blockchains could change the relationship of citizens with their government by bringing about more transparency and trustworthiness. But London has been very friendly to the technology since at least 2014. Many early blockchain startups incorporated or worked in London because it was the unofficially safest place to build a business. This was a big deal at that time because many cryptocurrency entrepreneurs were being arrested in 2014 and 2015.

Since this report came out, blockchains have been approved for use across government applications in the UK, including Whitehall departments (non-ministerial departments such as Land Registry, Forestry Commission, and Food Standards), local authorities, and delegated governments.

Here are several interesting projects and experiments that are happening in the UK:

>> **Blockchain-based welfare distribution:** The Department of Work and Pensions has partnered with Barclays, RWE, GovCoin, and the University of London in an experiment that will use blockchain technology to distribute welfare with a phone app. The trial was designed to see if payments could be sent and tracked using blockchain technology.

>> **Government DLT:** Credits, a blockchain platform provider, and the UK government are collaborating on a framework that allows UK government agencies to experiment with blockchain technology. (DLT stands for distributed ledger technology.)

>> **Blockchain-based international payments:** Santander Bank has launched a trial of blockchain-based international payments. The staff pilot program involves an app that connects to Apple Pay. Users can use touch ID to transfer payments of between £10 and £10,000.

>> **Using blockchain technology to trade gold:** The Royal Mint has teamed up with CME Group, a market operator, to use blockchain technology to build a gold market in the hopes of making London a more appealing city for gold sales. Blockchain technology is being adopted by the two entities because they see it as an efficient digital mechanism for trading gold.

These are all experiments to see if blockchain technology is the new platform to exchange value. The success or failure of this scheme will define the future course of the UK and the rest of the world.

The regulatory sandbox of Singapore

Singapore, like the UK, has gone out of its way to make working there as easy, friendly, and financially appealing as possible. In 2015, government officials traveled to San Francisco to announce and recruit entrepreneurs to come work in what they coined a "regulatory sandbox" — a play on the term *development sandbox*, which is a safe environment where developers can build software. Singapore had the same idea in mind for building software companies.

At that time, blockchain companies in the United States and many other places were still in the gray zone. The idea of a safe place to operate and invest money was very appealing to many entrepreneurs, myself included. If you've never been to Singapore, you should go! It's beautiful, clean, and safe.

Singapore is taking steps to explore the technology, and it's paying off. A Singaporean bank, OCBC, used blockchain technology for cross-border transfers. It sent money to its subsidiaries, OCBC Malaysia and the Bank of Singapore.

R3 has also been active in Singapore. It opened an lab for researching and developing digital ledger technologies alongside Monetary Authority of Singapore. R3 is working on an exchange to support interbank payments. The banks will deposit cash and be issued a digital currency.

Singapore's central bank also launched a pilot project, along with eight foreign and local banks as well as the stock exchange. This proof-of-concept project aims to use the blockchain technology for its interbank payments. The pilot project also aims to review cross-border foreign currency transactions.

It's not just blockchain companies that are going to experiment in Singapore. All the biggest players have gotten involved — Bank of America, Merrill Lynch, IBM, Credit Suisse, The Bank of Tokyo-Mitsubishi UFJ Ltd, DBS Bank Ltd, JP Morgan, The Hong Kong and Shanghai Banking Corp Ltd, OCBC Bank, United Overseas Bank, and the Singapore Exchange.

TIP

Every bank in the world must know who it's doing business with. The whole idea of know your customer (KYC) helps combat money laundering and tourist funding.

The next phase will be determining foreign currency transactions and building on Singapore's KYC efforts. This could lead to the country forging the way in blockchain-based identity. Singapore already has a robust and modern digital identity system that could easily be connected to a blockchain.

The Dubai 2020 initiative

The government of Dubai has an ambitious plan to move all government documents and systems onto the blockchain by 2020. The scheme to go paperless is part of its initiative to become a global leader in blockchain technology and boost efficiency across all sectors.

The Minister of Cabinet Affairs and the Future detailed how the new scheme will enable users to update and verify their credentials through the blockchain. They'll only have to log in with their credentials once to have access to both government and private entities, such as insurance companies and banks. They also anticipate sharing their technology with other countries to allow simpler border crossings.

Instead of passports, travelers could use pre-authenticated digital wallets, as well as pre-approved identification.

The Dubai government has estimated that its blockchain initiative has the potential to save 25.1 million hours in productivity. This boost in efficiency will also help to cut back on carbon emissions.

Dubai's Global Blockchain Council (GBC) announced seven new public-private collaborations, combining the skills and resources of startups, local businesses, and government departments. They'll apply blockchain technology to the following:

» **Healthcare:** The Estonian software company, Guardtime will collaborate with one of Dubai's largest telecom operators, Du, to provide the technological expertise for digitizing healthcare records and moving them to the blockchain.

» **The diamond trade:** A pilot project will use blockchain technology for the authentication and transfer of diamonds. The Dubai Multi Commodities Center will be digitize *Kimberly certificates* (documents created by the UN to restrict the trade of conflict diamonds).

» **Title transfers:** Title transfers will be digitized and recorded on a blockchain. A Singaporean blockchain startup known as Dxmarkets has developed a proof-of-concept.

» **Business registration:** The GBC is trialing the use of blockchain technology for business registration. This is different from the decentralized autonomous organization (DAO) of Ethereum but could streamline identity verification through the Flexi Desk program. It's currently in the demo stage, with several entities working on a proof-of-concept.

» **Tourism:** Dubai Points is a pilot program that was launched in collaboration with Loyyal, using blockchain technology to help the tourism industry. It aims to incentivize travel by granting points to travelers who visit certain places. It will use smart contracts to facilitate the rewards. These points many work like a crypto token and be tradable an exchanges.

» **Shipping:** IBM is working with the GBC to use blockchain technology for improved shipping and logistics. The program aims to help regional players to collaborate on how they exchange goods. Smart contracts will be utilized as solutions for compliance and settlement issues.

Dubai, like Singapore, has put its money and talent into insuring that it will dominate the blockchain space quickly. This is one luxury of small government and central authority.

Bitlicense regulatory framework: New York City

If you're planning on operating a blockchain startup in New York City, plan for extra fees. In June 2015, the New York State Department of Financial Services (NYDFS) put out the final version of Bitlicense, the regulatory framework for digital currency aimed to give the industry more clarity. In reality, it pushed many blockchain startups out of NYC. The license itself costs $5,000 and can be up to 500 pages. It requires the fingerprints of each company's leaders and an extensive background check on the applying businesses. The chief complaint is the roughly $100,000 in expenses associated with the application. This estimate includes time allocation, legal, and compliance fees. Bitlicense is in stark contrast to the efforts made by other financial centers such and London, Singapore, and Dubai.

The final Bitlicense was the result of almost two years of research and debate over how the technology should be regulated. It came about after it was deemed that the existing regulations were not suitable for digital currency companies.

On a positive note, NYC blockchain businesses no longer need approval from the NYDFS for new software updates or further rounds of venture capital funding. The framework states that digital currency firms only need approval for changes that are "proposed to an existing product, service, or activity that may cause such product, service, or activity to be materially different from that previously listed on the application for licensing by the superintendent."

The first company to receive a Bitlicense was Circle, the Bitcoin wallet providers. The license allows them to operate in New York under the regulatory framework. Circle is one of the few companies that can legally do so. Most blockchain startups are avoiding working in New York because the cost and effort of the license outweigh the benefit. Only the highest-funded startups are making an effort.

Ripple has been awarded its second license. This iteration of their license has allowed it to sell and hold XRP, which is the digital asset behind the Ripple Consensus Ledger (RCL). It will enhance Ripple's ability to deal with business customers who want to use its technology for international funds transfers.

Other U.S. regions have also put up similar bills to regulate digital currency and require licensing. California bill AB 1326, would have done that for the region but failed after the Electronic Frontier Foundation (EFF) was able to oppose it. (The EFF is a group based in San Francisco that defends consumer rights and new technology.)

Securing the World's Borders

Blockchain is being explored by many governments to secure borders. The UK has an ambitious goal of ensuring that travelers never need to break stride as they move through their airports. This is in contrast to the long security lines that are present now at almost every airport. The main hurdles that the UK must overcome for frictionless travel experience have to do with *passenger resolution* (the ability to know definitively any given passenger's identity, even if the passenger is from another country). Passenger resolution has been a problem for countries that are fighting terrorism.

The United States has opened up its technology for passenger resolution under the Global Travel Assessment System (GTAS). It's available for public collaboration on GitHub (www.github.com/US-CBP/GTAS).

Computers, cameras, and sensors involved in the noninvasive screening and authentication of passengers all need to be secured to ensure national security. Blockchains, with their underlying immutable properties, are a promising technology for this use case and are being tested now.

The other interesting thing that can be created through blockchains is biographical identities — identities that are built over time. Any data can be linked with a biographical identity, and the privacy and readability of the attributed data can be managed by publishers. Over time, identity is built by adding additional attributes. Attributes can be just about anything, from data off your personal device to instances that your documents were checked at a border crossing. These attributes are published to the individual's chain of identity by certificate authorities or those authorized by certificate authorities.

The Department of Homeland Security and the identity of things

The Department of Homeland Security under the Science and Technology Directorate is exploring securing IoT devices for the U.S. borders. It's working with Factom, Inc., an Austin, Texas–based blockchain startup to advance the security of digital identity for IoT devices.

Factom creates identity logs that captures the ID of a device, who manufactured it, lists of available updates, known security issues, and granted authorities while adding the dimension of time for added security. The goal is to limit would-be hackers' abilities to corrupt the past records for a device, making it harder to spoof.

Passports of the future

ShoCard (www.shocard.com) is an application development company that is working with the blockchain company Blockcypher. It has built prototypes that allow you to establish your identity within a secure blockchain environment. ShoCard ID lives on an app on your phone and can be used to share all different kinds of credentials securely.

The new feeder document

You may not have heard of Smartrac, but it's more than likely that you touch a piece of its technology every day. Smartrac is the number-one provider of radio-frequency identification (RFID) tags and other identification chips that live inside of things like passports and ID cards.

One of the largest challenges that countries face while fighting identity fraud is in the authentication of the underlying documents used to build identities. These are things like Social Security cards, birth certificates, and diplomas, which are currently easy and cheap to knock off.

Smartrac has been battling this problem with more and more sophisticated technology. Its latest innovation, dLoc, is a software authentication solution that allows feeder documents to be checked against a blockchain record.

Document data is married to a unique ID of the near-field communication tag (NFC) to create a 32-bit hash value, which is only recognizable by the issuing agency using a private key. The hash value is stored in Smart Cosmos and backed up in a public blockchain. After that has happened, the document with the dLoc sticker can be verified using a desktop reader or a mobile app on an NFC-enabled phone.

What this does is create a two amazing things that have never been possible with paper documents:

>> An unalterable history of the document, showing its true age and ownership.

>> Allowing certificate authorities to sign for the authenticity of a document cryptographically. So, even if the underlying paper used to create documents was stolen, it would not be adequately signed, or if a document was taken after it was issued, it could be marked as a stolen document.

world

» **Getting a head start on improved Internet infrastructure layers for your business and home**

» **Starting to make your own blockchain identity**

» **Monetizing your information through smart contracts**

Chapter 16

Other Industries

t's easy to focus on the most prominent blockchain projects and industry impacts, but blockchain technology has already begun to touch all aspects of society.

In this chapter, I lead you through some of the more interesting and unusual applications of blockchain technology that you may not have suspected. Some of the most exciting transformations will occur within government systems, new trust layers for the Internet, and new industries created by blockchains. Here, you discover the most impressive changes that are taking place now and how these transformations will affect your life and the industry you work in, as well as the governments and agencies that protect you.

Lean Governments

A few small nations have realized that if they are going to compete in a global economy, they have to offer more and do it in a way that does not burden their citizens. In order to compete, they've shifted many of the traditional ideas around what it means to provide citizenship. In a world that is moving from hard borders to very porous ones, where people have the power to choose where they live and what country they call home, these small countries are doing well.

Citizenship is becoming a commodity that can be purchased, with each nation offering different advantages. Countries are moving away from the passive citizenship model, where you're born a citizen of a country, to one where you choose citizenship based on the advantages that that country offers.

Under this new model, citizenship is no longer tied to a physical location. Government can exist without borders or a physical location. Old models see citizenship as a location that can be invaded and overruled by another nation or sources within, such as a revolution.

Blockchain technology and other top-grade innovations are being embraced in these areas — first, because they makes it possible and, second, because they help reduce the weight on government by creating more efficient systems that citizens can access quickly anywhere in the world, even if the physical territory is overrun.

Singapore, Estonia, and China have all been market leaders in these types of initiatives. The Smart Nation project of Singapore and e-Residency of Estonia are unique systems that strive to reduce the paperwork and wait times of citizens and increase the efficiency of shared resources. China's efforts to reduce fraud have changed the dynamics for the blockchain space.

Singapore's Smart Nation project

Smart Nation is Singapore's national effort to create a future of better living for all its citizens and inhabitants. People, businesses, and government are working together. The project spans from digital identity all the way to IoT sensors that optimize public records.

Singapore believes that people empowered by technology can lead more meaningful and fulfilled lives. It's exploiting new technologies, networks, and big data to its fullest and actively seeking innovation through regulator sandboxes and active recruitment and incentivizing innovation by startups.

You can see a depiction of the Smart Nation initiative at https://goo.gl/EGmF4X.

Singapore has been able to quickly test and deploy new technology because it has a single layer government. It coordinates policies and efforts across institutions quickly. Smart Nation is an excellent example of this philosophy that new technology trumps politics as usual.

Estonia's e-Residency

Estonia is a small country in the European Union with 1.3 million inhabitants. It has limited resources to meet the needs of its citizens, but through technology, it has been able to exceed the capabilities of many larger nations. Estonia launched digital ID cards for online services and was the first country to offer *e-Residency*, a digital identity, available to anyone in the world interested in operating a business online.

Signing up for an Estonia e-Residency takes a few minutes, and the background check costs about $100. Having an e-Residency card does not make you a citizen of Estonia, but it does give you a lot of benefits.

TIP

You can also become an Estonia e-Resident. Apply online at `https://apply.gov.ee`.

After it exited the Soviet Union, Estonia invested heavily in new technology. It shifted completely away from traditional government to one where it utilizes a *single-window principle* (one point of access for citizens). The single-window principle enables access to all tax and customs services for citizens with a single secure log-in anywhere in the world. Straightforward and paper-free transactions are made possible through this system. Everything, except marriage and real estate purchases, can be done completely online. Estonian citizens can make bank transfers or pay tax in a few minutes.

The Estonian people have come to expect their government to simplify and use more IT solutions. The active development of e-services has reduced the number of visits to the Estonian Tax and Customs Board service bureaus by more than 60 percent between 2009 and 2016, lowering the overall cost.

Estonia upgraded its income and social tax returns environment in 2015 and collected €125 million more in value-added tax (VAT) than the previous year due to the development and extensive usage of e-services. The Estonian government added a tax liability calculator that pulls data from incorporated banking systems of citizens. It also made it easy to submit invoices to the system.

The Estonians have embraced blockchain technologies. The next big development will be a blockchain-enabled cloud. Estonia has hired Ericsson, Apcera, and Guardtime to jointly develop and operate a hybrid cloud platform that will enhance the scalability, resilience, and data security of tax reporting and online health care advice.

Nasdaq is developing blockchain services in Estonia as well. It's building a market for private companies that keeps track of the shares they issue and enables them to settle transactions immediately. It's focused on improving the proxy voting process for enterprises. It will be a way to register your business.

The Bitnation project is collaborating with Estonia to offer a public notary to Estonian e-Residents, which will allow Estonia's e-Residents, regardless of where they live or do business, to notarize their marriages, birth certificates, and business contracts on a blockchain. Blockchain notarized documents aren't legally binding in the Estonian jurisdiction, or in any other nation or state, but it will allow citizens to prove the age of these documents.

Better notarization in China

China has a love–hate relationship with cryptocurrency. On the one hand, Chinese citizens have been trying to use tokens as a means to launder money out of the country or hide profits from taxation. This has caused the Chinese government to tighten regulation around the use of cryptocurrencies. However, as the usefulness of the underlying blockchain technology has expanded beyond the movement of value, China has begun to embrace blockchain technology.

An interesting example of its early use was by Ancun Zhengxin Co., which is leading the shift to electronic data notarization services in China through partnerships with more than 100 traditional notarial offices in 28 provinces. It's also offering electronic data storage and blockchain notarization solution through traditional offices.

Ancun publishes thousands of records in a publicly searchable blockchain that allow users to go back and check the authenticity and age of notarized documents.

Many startups are working on similar concepts in the United States. For example, Tierion (www.tierion.com) lets you hash and timestamp date; it anchors the data for you in the Bitcoin blockchain.

The Trust Layer for the Internet

Over the last 30 years, the Internet has been built in layers — one layer on top of the next — making it easier and safer for the those using it. The blockchain is the next layer of the Internet. Think of it as the trust layer. It will likely fade quietly out of the public's consciousness and just start making your online interactions more pleasant. The implementation of blockchain technology will eventually do away with irritating problems that commonly occur online because there aren't sufficient ways to trust information.

There are two key areas where work has begun that you may not be aware of but will love: email with little to no spam and a new kind of identity online.

Spam-free email

You likely hate spam as much as I do, but there is a bigger problem than too many unwanted emails. The current email systems are no longer secure. At the end of 2016, Yahoo! suffered one of the world's largest hacks. One billion user accounts were compromised, and users' personal data was exposed.

Securing email is a compelling use case for blockchain technology, and email is ready to be disrupted. A legend in online security has taken on the challenge. Dr. John McAfee, the antivirus software pioneer, has created a new platform for email based on blockchain technology.

John McAfee SwiftMail (www.johnmcafeeswiftmail.com) is a blockchain-based email. It isn't that different from the email systems you're used to. It's easy to navigate, and some developers have built mobile apps and web-based apps to make the experience more convenience.

SwiftMail's blockchain confirms that your mail is genuine and that the emails you send were received by the intended parties, removing the need to trust a third party, like Yahoo!, with your data. There is also a small inherent cost to send an email that desensitizes spammers.

SwiftMail takes a strong stance on privacy where many service providers have a blasé attitude. John McAfee says, "If privacy doesn't matter, would you be willing to give your wallet to a total stranger and let them go through it and write down everything they find inside? Then why on earth would we believe that if we're not doing anything wrong, we shouldn't care if someone has our information?"

SwiftMail uses wallet address similar to a Bitcoin wallet that is kept on an application on your computer. They are 32 random characters with no metadata to scrap, and users can create new ones quickly, just as you do with Bitcoin. The emails themselves are 256-bit, end-to-end encryption making intercepted data useless to thieves.

REMEMBER

Currently, downloads for SwiftMail are only available for Android, Linux and Windows systems. There is no Apple-friendly version of this software yet. Don't download the wrong version.

Other projects in this space, including 21 (www.21.co), are working on giving email a blockchain backend. They've created email that charges people outside your network a fee to send you email. Then they give you the option to keep the money or donate it to charity.

Owning your identity

One of the fundamental tenets that blockchain enthusiast talks about is the personal responsibility of owning the data that you create and that identifies you uniquely. This concept might seem straightforward, but most people don't own or control the data that represents their identities.

Most of the control is held by centralized databases that are vulnerable to hacking. These databases hold the information, and certificate authorities validate that the information is correct and unaltered. In the information age, your data is your identity. The more distributed the data is, the higher the likelihood that it will fall into the hands of those who want to misuse it.

Blockchain-based identity places control of identity in the hands of the individuals or corporations that that the identity represents. Central databases and certificate authorities are not necessarily replaced. Data still needs a secure home, and it still makes sense to have third parties validate the authenticity of documents.

The value in changing the order of responsibility around identity is that it becomes harder to steal, hold hostage, or manipulate the underlying documents that represent your identity. Information is shared as needed without exposing unnecessary information.

Oracle of the Blockchain

Blockchain technology doesn't solve for the problem that information must come from somewhere. It's also important that the information can be relied on. It's the human element that can't yet be removed from the equation when you want to act on a contract within a blockchain system.

There is no central authority to police or enforce honesty in a blockchain system. Predicting the future honesty of authors of information is impossible. The logical conclusion is that each transaction must cost less than the cost to rebuild reputation. The reputations of trusted authors are built over time, and the longer an author is honest and correct, the more valuable the author's reputation becomes. This concept is similar to the value of a name brand.

In this section, I explain how artists and creatives are using blockchain technology to monetize their work through blockchain technology.

Trusted authorship

Smart contracts and chain codes have created a new opportunity for knowledgeable individuals and corporations to monetize their information. These types of systems need trusted sources of information to execute against. These trusted sources could be rating agencies, weather outlets, or just about anything else.

You could also connect IoT devices to a blockchain infrastructure and have them create their own voices and identities on a blockchain network. They need to build trust over time and can still be corrupted at any given point. Past honesty doesn't prevent future dishonesty or the corruption of a source of information.

Not all smart contracts or chain codes are self-contained or execute against infallible sources. The more practical and applicable business use case requires information to be derived from sources outside the known universe of any given blockchain network. Several startups are attacking this problem from different angles.

Factom has created Acolyte, a service that allows users to build a reputation over time for the information they provide to the network. Smart contract builders can subscribe and compensate oracles that are created. They can also rate them for their trustworthiness.

From a dramatically different angle, Augur, another blockchain startup, has pioneered the idea of prediction markets. Augur is a platform that rewards users for predicting future real-world events such as election or corporate buyouts. The bets are made by trading virtual shares in the outcome of events. Users make money by buying shares in the correct outcomes. The cost of the shares fluctuates based on how the community feels about the likelihood of the event acutely happening. Augur is similar to a betting website. Anyone can make a prediction. Anyone can create a prediction market for any given event. This would allow you as a business owner, for example, to take a poll on what people think is most likely to occur. It may also uncover inside information that authors would like to be able to capitalize on.

Intellectual property rights

One of the hardest-hit industries that is struggling with intellectual property rights is the music industry. Artists at the top are squeezed out economically by the many intermediaries that rely on their creative work. Small artists can't make music a primary source of income because they only see a small fraction of the revenue. Mega-stars make it on the sheer volume of fans.

The Internet has made it easier for artists of all sizes to share their work. At the same time, it has made it even harder for people to make a comfortable living doing what they love. The music industry food chain is a long, and each intermediary takes a small piece of the pie and adds to the length of time that it takes for funds to finally reach the artist. Often, the artist will wait up to 18 months or more to see any money and may only get $0.000035 per instance of her music being streamed. This situation is a best-case scenario in our current market, with no one defrauding the artist.

Blockchain has been introduced as a way to help lighten the massive financial burden on creatives. Cryptocurrency could be used to reduce transaction fees associated with credit cards and fraud. It would also open up new markets in developing countries that don't have regular access to credit cards.

An even more interesting but less straightforward possibility would be migrating the whole music industry ecosystem onto a blockchain system that utilized smart contracts or chain code to facilitate immediate payment for utilization. It could also clarify ownership of licenses and make it easier for consumers to license music for commercial use.

Several projects are working on this issue and looking to promote a healthy, sustainable, and frictionless ecosystem — one that does not displace market player but does allow artists to gain a bit more from their hard work.

UjoMusic is beta testing its platform that lets users sell and license music directly. It utilizes the Ethereum network, smart contracts for execution, and Ether (the Ethereum cryptocurrency) for payment. You can download a whole song or just the vocal and instrumental stems for commercial or noncommercial use. The musicians are then paid immediately with Ether.

Peertracks is another blockchain startup that's working on changing the music industry. It's a music streaming website that allows users to download and discover new artists. It does this through its peer-to-peer network called MUSE and the creation of individual artist tokens. These tokens work like other cryptocurrency and fluctuate in value depending on the popularity of the artist.

Blockchain technology doesn't remove the need for music labels and distributors. However, they'll need to act quickly if they don't want to be displaced by new companies that adapt this more efficient model, just as Netflix disrupted Blockbuster.

5

The Part of Tens

Chapter **17**

Ten Free Blockchain Resources

In this chapter, I outline interesting free resources across the blockchain ecosystem that will help you stay informed and get involved in the community. Here, you can find free tools for making *oracles* (the data feeds that allow smart contracts to execute), videos that will expand your knowledge, and organizations that are shaping the future of the industry.

Factom University

Factom, Inc., is a blockchain company that services the Factom open-source network. It builds custom blockchain applications for large corporations and governments. It has also built a blockchain as a service product for the U.S. mortgage industry.

Factom University (www.factom.com/university) was created by Factom, Inc., and is a growing knowledge base created to teach individuals about blockchain technology, the Factom platform, and APIs. It consists of videos and tutorials that will take you from novice to expert. Factom University has plans to launch a certificate program, so stay tuned!

Ethereum 101

Ethereum is an open-source crowdfunded project that built the Ethereum block-chains. It's one of the most important projects in the space because it has pioneered building a programing language within a blockchain. Due to its built-in programing language, the Ethereum network allows you to create smart contracts, create decentralized organizations, and deploy decentralized applications.

Ethereum 101 (www.ethereum101.org) is a website started by the members of the Ethereum community. It's a curated repository for high-quality educational content about blockchain technology and the Ethereum network. Anthony D'Onofrio, Ethereum's Director of Community, oversees the project.

Build on Ripple

Ripple provides global financial settlement solutions. Its distributed settlement network is built on open-source technology that anyone can use. Ripple cautions that its blockchain capabilities should only be used by licensed financial institutions.

Ripple has developed a robust knowledge base for building on its platform (www.ripple.com/build). This knowledge base is geared primarily for developers. Ripple also offers some resources for financial regulators. It's worth a read even if you aren't a regulator, because it gives some insight into legal liabilities that come up with blockchain technology.

Programmable Money by Ripple

Steven Zeiler is a Ripple employee who developed a YouTube series on how to create programmable money on the Ripple network using JavaScript. This series is geared for JavaScript programmers. As of this writing, there are ten videos that will talk you through development. Check out the YouTube series at https://goo.gl/g8vFPL.

DigiKnow

DigiByte is a decentralized payment network inspired by Bitcoin. It allows you to move money over the Internet and offers faster transactions and lower fees than Bitcoin. The network is also open to those who want to mine its native token.

The founder of DigiByte, Jared Tate, created a video series on YouTube, called DigiKnow, that teaches you just about everything you need to know to utilize DigiByte. Here is a link to his first video, where he walks you through the basics of how blockchains work and how the DigiByte network adds value: https://youtu.be/scr6BzFddso.

Blockchain University

Blockchain University is an educational website that teaches developers, manager, and entrepreneurs about the blockchain ecosystem. It offers public and private training programs, hackathons, and demo events. Its programs are solution-oriented design thinking and hands-on experiential training. You can find Blockchain University in Mountain View, California, or at http://blockchainu.co.

Bitcoin Core

Bitcoin Core (https://bitcoin.org) was originally used by Satoshi Nakamoto to host his whitepaper on Bitcoin protocol. It's home to educational material on Bitcoin core protocol and downloadable versions of the original Bitcoin software.

The site is dedicated to keeping Bitcoin decentralized and accessible to the average person.

REMEMBER

It's a community-run project, and not all the content is managed by the core team. Keep this in mind while perusing the site.

Blockchain Alliance

The Blockchain Alliance was founded by the Blockchain Chamber of Digital Commerce and the news organization Coincenter. It's a public-private collaboration by the blockchain community, law enforcement, and regulators. They share a common goal to make the blockchain ecosystem more secure and to promote further development of technology. They do this by combat criminal activity on the blockchain by providing education, technical assistance, and periodic informational sessions regarding Bitcoin and other digital currencies and those utilize blockchain technology.

You can learn more about their events or join their organization at www.blockchainalliance.org.

Multichain Blog

Multichain is a company that helps organizations rapidly build applications on blockchains. They offer a platform that can issue millions of assets on a private blockchain and you can also track and verify activity on your network through their tools. Beyond their toolset and platform, they've been thought leaders in the blockchain space.

These are my favorite posts from their blog (www.multichain.com/blog):

>> Four genuine blockchain use cases (www.multichain.com/blog/2016/05/four-genuine-blockchain-use-cases/)

>> Beware the impossible smart contract (www.multichain.com/blog/2016/04/beware-impossible-smart-contract/)

>> Smart contracts and the DAO implosion (www.multichain.com/blog/2016/06/smart-contracts-the-dao-implosion/)

>> Understanding zero knowledge blockchains (www.multichain.com/blog/2016/11/understanding-zero-knowledge-blockchains/)

HiveMind

Paul Sztorc founded Truthcoin, a peer-to-peer oracle system and prediction marketplace for Bitcoin. It utilizes a proof-of-work sidechain that stores data on the state of prediction markets. Bitcoin can support financial derivatives and smart contracts through HiveMind, the platform developed out of the Truthcoin whitepaper. Check out their resources and education materials at http://bitcoinhivemind.com.

Chapter **18**

The Ten Rules to Never Break on the Blockchain

In this chapter, I dig into the things you should take into account while working with blockchain technology and the cryptocurrencies that run them.

REMEMBER

Always consult your CPA and attorney before making financial decisions. This technology is new, and the rules that govern it are not fully developed.

Don't Use Cryptocurrency or Blockchains to Skirt the Law

The legality and the legal zoning of cryptocurrencies are still fluctuating in many places of the world. I'm not kidding when I tell you to talk to your CPA and your attorney. It will be money well spent and will keep you out of trouble.

Here are three very silly questions that I get asked frighteningly often:

>> **Can I use cryptocurrency as a way to hide money?** This idea is a dangerous one. *Remember:* Blockchains keep records of all transactions forever, so even if you think you came up with a clever way to hide some tokens, those looking for bad behavior have time to find it.

>> **Can I use blockchains as a way to smuggle money out of my country?** Many countries have limitations on the funds citizens can take out of the country. You don't want to do this for the same reason as I just mentioned: Blockchains keep records of all transactions forever.

>> **Can I use cryptocurrency to buy illicit goods?** The answer is — you guessed it — no! Blockchains keep a trail of your actions *forever!*

REMEMBER

Don't do anything with cryptocurrency and blockchains that would be illegal to do with real money.

Keep Your Contracts as Simple as Possible

Decentralized autonomous organizations (DAOs), smart contracts, and chaincode are all the rage at the moment. The promise of cutting administration and legal cost is very enticing to many corporations. A sometimes overlooked characteristic of this technology is that it is just code. That means that there is no human being interpreting the rules that you've laid out for everyone to follow. The code becomes law, and the law only stretches to what is incorporated into the blockchain contract. The "fat" that was cut can sometimes be very important.

There is no one to interpret the code. That means that if the code is executed in a fashion that you did not expect, there is also no one to enforce the intent of the contract. The code is law and nothing unlawful occurred. That's why you should to keep your contracts simple and modular in nature to contain and predict the outcomes of contract fulfillment. It's also a good idea to have your contract tested and beaten up even by other developers who are incentivized to break it.

The reach of the blockchain you're building your project on matters, too. You can think of it like jurisdictions. Sure, a smart contract can execute on outside data, but the smart contract cannot demand funds from accounts that they do not have access to. That means that all the value must be set aside in some manner, which may encumber cash flow.

Another thing to think about is the source of information that your contract uses to execute against. If it's weather data for an insurance contract, do you trust and agree on the source? Is it possible to manipulate the source data? A lot of thought should go into the oracle source before implementation.

Publish with Great Caution

The whole point of blockchains is that once data is put in, it's hard to take it out. That means that what you put in will be around for a long time. If you publish encrypted sensitive information, you need to be okay with the fact that the encrypted data may one day be broken and what you published may be readable to anyone.

TIP

Think about this before you publish:

>> Would I be comfortable with this information being decrypted at some point?

>> Am I comfortable sharing this information for all eternity with anyone who wants to review it?

>> Is this data harmful to a third party and something that I could be liable for if published?

There is work being done in cryptography to make quantum proof encryption, but because both quantum computing and quantum proof encryption are still in the testing phase, it's difficult to say what the technology will be capable of 20 years from now.

Back Up, Back Up, Back Up Your Private Keys

REMEMBER

Blockchains are very unforgiving creatures. They don't care if you lost your private keys or passwords. Many a crypto nerd has been laid bare and given up countless tokens to the great blockchain oceans — treasure that will never be recovered.

The private keys that control your cryptocurrency often live inside your wallets, so it's important to protect and secure them. Be careful with online services that store your money for you. Many cryptocurrency exchanges and online wallets have had their funds stolen.

TIP

Only store small amounts of tokens for everyday use online or in an Internet-accessible device. Think of cryptocurrency wallets like your cash wallet. Don't keep more money in it than you're willing to lose at any given time. More than a hundred known malware applications are looking to get ahold of your private keys and steal your tokens.

Keep the rest of your currency in *cold storage* — completely offline with zero access to the Internet. This could be in a paper wallet, on a computer that can't access the Internet, or in a unique hardware device built for securing cryptocurrency.

If you choose to use a paper wallet to secure your cryptocurrency, laminate it and make copies. Also keep in mind that printers often have access to the Internet and their data can be retrieved by third parties. The truly paranoid only use printers that have no access to the web. Keep your paper wallet copies in different locations such as a bank vault and a secure location in your home.

REMEMBER

Back up your digital wallets and store them in a safe place. A backup is in case your computer fails, or you make a mistake and delete the wrong file. The backup will allow you to recover your wallet in case your device was corrupted or stolen. Also, don't forget to encrypt your wallet. Encrypting your wallet allows you to set a password for withdrawing tokens.

TOOLS TO KEEP YOUR TOKENS SAFE

You might consider using the BitGo wallet to secure your Bitcoin. Although it is an online wallet, BitGo requires both an online and offline signature to move your tokens. Because of this functionality, it's more secure than your standard online wallet.

BitGo wallets use three keys. They hold one, you hold one, and the other is held on your behalf by a third-party key recovery service (KRS). Two signatures are required on every transaction. Usually this is done by BitGo and you, unless you lose one of your keys; in that case, the KRS will help out. The BitGo wallet is not free — they require a small fee per transaction.

Check out the BitGo wallet at www.bitgo.com/wallet.

WARNING

Encryption is a helpful measure to protect you against thieves, but it can't shield you against keylogging software. Always use a secure password that contains letters, numbers, punctuation marks, and is at least 16 characters long. The most secure passwords are those generated by programs designed specifically for that purpose. Strong passwords are harder to remember. You might consider writing down your password and laminating it like your private keys. There are limited password recovery options within cryptocurrency, and a forgotten password could mean lost tokens.

Triple-Check the Address Before Sending Currency

Cryptocurrency has attracted a fair number of scoundrels, so be careful when you send money. As soon as the money is out of your wallet, it's gone forever, and there is no way to get it back. There are no chargebacks and you can't call customer support. Your money is gone.

Triple-check the wallet address before sending. You want to make sure you're sending it to the right address.

Take Care When Using Exchanges

Cryptocurrency exchanges are central points that hackers like to target to steal tokens. They're seen as pots of gold just ripe for the picking, and more than 150 of them have been compromised.

Keep this in mind while using exchanges, and follow the best practices laid out in this book to keep your tokens safe. Do a little research on the exchange you're using to see what security measures it has in place.

Finally, just use exchanges to move your funds in and out. Don't use the exchange as a place to store value. Instead, hold significant amounts of crypto in cold storage or in a laminated paper wallet with several copies.

Beware Wi-Fi

If your router wasn't set up correctly, it's possible for someone to see a log of all your activity. If you're on a public network, assume that the owner of the network can see your activity.

WARNING

Only use trusted Wi-Fi networks and make sure you've changed the password on your router to something as secure as a password. Most Wi-Fi router passwords are set to a factory default of "admin" and can easily be taken over by a third party.

Identify Your Blockchain Dev

Blockchain technology is new, and there just aren't that many people who have a lot of experience when it comes to building blockchain applications.

If you're thinking about hiring a developer to help you with a project, check out her GitHub and see what work she's done before you get started. She may not need to be experienced with blockchain specifically, but if she isn't, she should be a very experienced developer outside of the blockchain world.

There aren't many resources out there yet to help developers when they get stuck. Inexperienced developers may struggle more and take longer to develop your application.

Don't Get Suckered

The blockchain industry as a whole does not have the same protection and security measures that banks and other financial institutions have, and there are not the same laws for your protection and financial welfare. There is no consumer protection and no FDIC bank insurance of funds from the government. If you get robbed or conned, you may not be able to turn to anyone for help.

Also, the industry has had a lot of hype in the last few years without much delivery of things of real value. The year 2016 saw over a thousand new blockchain companies pop up overnight claiming expertise. When you're looking at developing a project and trying to decide if it's worth the investment, it's always a good idea to take a minute and make sure it even makes sense. Ask yourself the following questions:

>> Is there real value generated?

>> Is the value created in the way that benefits you?

>> Are there other more tested technologies that could be used to accomplish the same thing with the same efficiency or better?

Blockchain technology holds a lot of promise and power and, as such, should be approached thoughtfully and carefully.

Don't Trade Tokens Unless You Know What You're Doing

Cryptocurrencies are very volatile and will swing wildly in value at any given time and sometimes for no discernable reason. Many of the cryptocurrencies have little depth, and trading large amounts can crash the market value. Working with published blockchains means that you'll likely need to hold some amount of the currency to utilize them.

Don't get caught up in trading the tokens unless you take the time to understand the market well. If you do choose to trade the tokens, don't forget to report this activity to your CPA. You may need to report your gains or loses on your income tax return.

Chapter **19**

Ten Top Blockchain Projects

N ew blockchain startups are emerging every day. Entrepreneurs have seen opportunities to capitalize on the very powerful tools blockchains offer to move money faster, secure computer systems, and build digital identities.

In this chapter, I introduce you to some of my favorite projects and companies. After reading this chapter, you'll have an idea of some of the amazing things happening within the blockchain software space. You may even get some ideas about what you could do yourself!

The R3 Consortium

Many banks have invested in building blockchain prototypes — many for Know Your Customer (KYC) requirements for anti-money laundering and prototypes for reducing the cost of exchanging money. They have to overcome several challenges, including the security of private information and the regulatory gray zone of cryptocurrencies.

R3 (www.r3cev.com) is an innovative company that has built a consortium with more than 75 of the world's leading financial institutions to integrate and take advantage of new blockchain technology. R3 is improving cross-border exchange, lowering the cost of auditing, and improving the speed of interbank fund transfer and settlement.

R3's three pillars are as follows:

>> **Financial-grade blockchain:** R3 has developed the base layer technology that supports a global financial institution's needs.

>> **Research and development:** R3 has created a bilateral research center that is testing and creating industry standards for commercial-grade blockchain technology.

>> **Product development:** R3 works in close collaboration with institutions to create products that solve problems up and down the value chain.

R3 has developed a blockchain platform for financial institutions called Corda. Corda is a distributed ledger platform designed to manage and synchronize financial agreements between regulated financial institutions. Unlike most blockchains that broadcast their transactions to the whole network, transactions may execute in parallel, on different nodes, without either node being aware of the other's transactions. The history of the network is on a need-to-know basis.

Key features of Corda include the following:

>> **Controlled access:** Only parties with a legitimate need to know can see the data.

>> **No central controller.**

>> **Regulatory and supervisory observer nodes.**

>> **Validation by parties to the transaction rather than a broader pool of unrelated validators.**

>> **Support for a variety of consensus mechanisms.**

>> **No native cryptocurrency.**

T ZERO: Overstocking the Stock Market

T ZERO is a platform that integrates blockchain technology with existing market processes to reduce settlement time and costs and increase transparency, efficiency, and auditability. T ZERO is able to do this because it's modular and adaptable.

T ZERO is a subsidiary of Overstock.com, focusing on the development and commercialization of fintech-based technologies based on cryptographically secured, decentralized ledgers. Since its inception in October 2014, T ZERO (`www.t0.com`) has established working commercial blockchain products.

It partnered with Keystone Capital Corporation, an independent broker-dealer located in California to create the first public issuance of blockchain equities. Together they provide brokerage services for users that trade blockchain securities.

Patrick Byrne, Overstock's founder and CEO, led this initiative. The opaque business practices of Wall Street have opened up market opportunities for a clear and trustworthy trading platform where consumers know what they're buying and the costs involved. The SEC declared parent company Overstock.com's S-3 filing effective, giving Overstock.com the ability to issue blockchain shares in a public offering. It also partnered with the Industrial and Commercial of Bank of China (ICBC), the world's largest bank, to test the platform.

Byrne achieves this through Medici, Overstock.com's majority-owned financial technology subsidiary. Medici focuses on applying blockchain technology to solving significant financial transaction problems. Its first initiative is to clean up securities settlement.

Blockstream's Distributed Systems

Blockstream (`www.blockstream.com`) has an excellent reputation in providing blockchain technologies and has a primary focus on distributed systems. Blockstream offers hardware and software solutions to organizations utilizing blockchain-based networks.

Blockstream Elements is the core software platform of the company and a segment of an open-source project. It offers several resources and a highly productive protocol for blockchain developers.

Blockstream's major field of innovation is in sidechains, which scale the utility of existing blockchains, enhancing their privacy and functionality by adding features like smart contracts and confidential transactions. Sidechains avoid liquidity shortages that many cryptocurrencies experience. Sidechains also permit digital assets to be transferred between different blockchains.

Sidechains make it possible to practically trade company shares on a blockchain without worrying about transaction cost or slow network speeds. Distributed asset management infrastructure can also leverage the Bitcoin network, permitting individuals and organizations to issue different asset classes.

Blockstream also has worked to create the Lightning Network, a system that lets Bitcoin support micropayment without slowing down the network. The Lightning Network support high volumes of small payments using proportional transaction fees and operating very fast. It's developing more Bitcoin Lightning prototypes and creating consensus and interoperability.

OpenBazaar's Blockchain

OpenBazaar (www.openbazaar.org) is an open-source project that built a decentralized network for peer-to-peer digital commerce. Instead of traditional models where buyers and sellers go through a centralized service, like Amazon or eBay, the OpenBazaar platform connects them directly. They also utilize Bitcoin's cryptocurrency to cut out fees and restrictions.

You need to download and install the OpenBazaar program on your computer. It then connects you to other people looking to buy and sell goods and services. It's a peer-to-peer network that is not controlled by any company or organization. After you download the app, it's easy to set yourself up as a buyer or seller. When you're ready to purchase something, just do a search and see what comes up. It's kind of like an anarchist's version of eBay.

OpenBazaar may sound a lot like Silk Road, but it isn't. Unlike on Silk Road, users are not anonymous. They can be tracked easily with their IP addresses, which makes it very unattractive for criminals. You can pull seller location data from the OpenBazaar API and map the position of all the participants in the network. There are a few ways to hide your location, and more private messaging is being explored, but currently, there is little to no illicit trade on the network.

OpenBazaar is working to appeal to major merchants and independent retailers. Those who can handle Bitcoin transactions and want to save money could gain a competitive advantage over the competition.

Code Valley: Find Your Coder

Code Valley (www.codevalley.com) takes the traditional model for developing code and turns it on its head. It describes itself as a "World Compiler." Code Valley provides developers with a marketplace tool to build software in collaboration with other developers via what Code Valley calls "agents."

Each agent within the system returns a fragment of code for the client's project. Code Valley also creates an open marketplace for entrepreneurs.

In Code Valley, clients, have access to a global network of developers who are willing and able to build software for them. Code Valley works similar to how online freelancer websites like Upwork operate. Developers in this system win opportunities to build software from the clients. The clients must, in turn, carefully select who can work on their projects.

Code Valley also works a little like a data access object (DAO) in that when a new project is created, it triggers the formation of a hidden and hivelike software compiler. The client's application is built collaboratively with the compiler by many different agents. Code Valley is industrializing software creation with blockchain technology.

Bitfury's Digital Assets

The Bitfury Group (www.bitfury.com) started out as a Bitcoin mining company, but it has transitioned into a full-service blockchain technology company. Bitfury develops software and creates hardware solutions for businesses and governments to move asset across the blockchains.

Bitfury is completely dedicated to the improvement of Bitcoin's blockchain ecosystem. Its technology helps in the efficient management of digital assets. It offers added security to private and public blockchain transactions using hardware and software solutions.

Bitfury processes private and public blockchain transactions. It also helps clients with blockchain analytics. Bitfury utilizes the immutable and always publicly viewable history of Bitcoin transactions and conducts advanced data analytics for transaction histories. Governments have used this type of work to track criminal activities across the Bitcoin blockchain.

Bitfury is also involved in the development of the Lightning Network. Lightning is an overlay network to Bitcoin's blockchain, enabling instantaneous micro transactions.

Bitfury is also working on a property rights registry. The Republic of Georgia has partnered with Bitfury to register land titles. The record of ownership is recorded in a blockchain to secure the history in an unalterable state. The safe transfer of property would be economically beneficial in the developing world.

Any Coin Can ShapeShift

ShapeShift (www.shapeshift.io) is one of the quickest ways to exchange block-chain assets and cryptocurrencies. Users are allowed to trade digital currencies within seconds using this service. The users don't have to worry about security — there is no login. Through its systems, ShapeShift significantly minimizes the risk of stolen tokens.

ShapeShift follows a strict "no fiat" policy. In the financial services industry, *fiat* does not refer to the cute little Italian car; instead, it's a way of differentiating government-issued currencies. On ShapeShift, users are not allowed to buy cryp-tocurrencies with bank accounts or debit or credit cards. ShapeShift can be used all over the world except in North Korea and New York State.

Using ShapeShift is very easy. You go to the website, specify the currency type you want to exchange, and specify what wallet to send the exchanged tokens to. ShapeShift exchanges the tokens for you, receives them into an account, and then sends them to the destination you specified.

Several market sources determine the exchange rate used by ShapeShift, and it always remains the same, independent of the value of currency exchanged. You can also convert Bitcoin and other cryptocurrencies directly within ShapeShift.

ShapeShift offers many unique features and tools like Shifty Button and Shape-Shift Lens, which allow users to purchase items with any alternative cryptocur-rency and receive and exchange altcoin payments directly and quickly.

Machine-Payable Apps on 21

21 Inc. (www.21.co) is one of the best-funded blockchain companies in the block-chain space with over $116 million raised. Andreessen Horowitz, Data Collective, Khosla Ventures, RRE Ventures, and Yuan Capital are among the venture capital firms contributed to 21.

21 is building software and hardware that makes it easy to work with Bitcoin over HTTP. It facilitates fast machine-to-machine payments. Users can send, receive, and implement micropayments over HTTP. 21 also allows users to write machine-payable apps on its system.

One of 21's devices is an embeddable mining chip, called BitShare. It can be embedded into an Internet-connected device as a standalone chip or integrated into an existing chipset as a block of IP. The BitShare generates a stream of digital currency for use in a wide variety of applications.

21 does four other things as well. It has

>> A downloadable app that is a fast way to get Bitcoin in any country, without a bank account or credit card

>> A marketplace where you can buy or sell API calls for Bitcoin with developers around the world, as well as add Bitcoin micropayments with one line of code

>> A dashboard that can monitor your Bitcoin earnings and network activity

>> A system that lets you connect with developers and host your machine-payable APIs

Anonymous Transactions on Dash

Dash (www.dash.org) is the first cryptocurrency modeled after Bitcoin. The developers of Dash wanted to add more privacy to their transactions. (On the Bitcoin network, anyone can review your transaction history.) So, Dash allows you to keep your funds and financial transactions private. It does this through a mixing protocol, which anonymizes transactions by mixing transactions of several parties, merging their funds together in a way where they can't be uncoupled. This is done through a decentralized network of servers called *masternodes*.

Dash plans to be the first protection-driven cryptographic cash with fully encoded exchanges and private block transactions. Dash debit cards can be utilized at any ATM around the world or in stores. They can also be designated into various monetary standards, such as dollars, euros, or pounds.

Dash has the following features:

>> **Privacy:** It keeps all your payments, transactions, and balances private so that nobody can track you.

>> **Speed:** It uses InstantX technology with a masternode network to complete transactions within seconds.

>> **Security:** Advanced encryption and trusted protocols make the system safe.

- **>> Global reach:** Darksend makes it a comprehensive system that enables you to send money worldwide quickly and anonymously.

- **>> Low fees:** The money transfer transactions cost only a few cents.

Dash also offers two wallets — an online version and one you can download to your computer.

ConsenSys: Decentralized Applications

ConsenSys (www.consensys.net) was created by one of the founders of Ethereum. It builds decentralized applications, enterprise blockchain solutions, and various developer tools for the Ethereum blockchain ecosystems.

ConsenSys is working with Microsoft to create an open-source blockchain identity system. This partnership came from the need set out by the United Nations ID2020, the goal of which is to curb crimes against humanity that come from a lack of identification. The plan is to have a legal identity for every person by the year 2020.

ConsenSys has developed the uPort identity solution, with integrated support for reputation systems and transactional security. The uPort system allows individuals to manage their identity elements in a portable and persistent manner on the Ethereum blockchain.

Users in less developed areas of the world can bootstrap their identities and reputations.

RepSys adds to the functionality of the uPort system. It enables people, organizations, and "things" to attest to the conduct of their counterparties on various kinds of transactions. Think of it sort of like Amazon reviews for identity. uPort holds the reputation attributes. These can both be official things like government-issued IDs, as well as Facebook pages. ConsenSys is also building in KYC solutions so that financial institutions can offer financial services.

Index

A

Abraham, Nikhil (author)
Coding For Dummies, 34, 107

Accenture, 100

Acolyte, 177

Active Directory (AD), 111, 116, 118

advantageous arbitrage transaction placement, as risk unique to Ripple, 72

Africa
as not having landlines or addresses, 138
trade of with China, 137–138
trends in blockchain technology in, 149

AI (artificial intelligence), 58, 119, 122, 143

algorithms
for creating agreement, 12
DigiByte as using five separate, 89, 91, 93
Groestl, 91
Qubit, 91
Scrypt, 91
SHA-256, 10, 86, 91, 94
Skein, 91
Sumeragi, 104–105

altcoin exchange platform, 14

altcoin prices, 78

Amazon.com, for mining equipment, 49

Ancun Zhengxin Co., 174

Andhara Pradesh (India), 161

Andreesen Horowitz, 66, 198

Andresen, Gavin (Bitcoin developer), 45

anti-money laundering (AML) regulations, 54, 133, 135, 165, 193

Apcera, 173

APIs (application programming interfaces), 81

Apollo, 81

app development, 105–106

app-activated payments, 134

Apple Pay, 164

application programming interfaces (APIs), 81

application-specific integrated circuit (ASIC), 93

arbitrage, 72

Aribnb, 160

artificial intelligence (AI), 58, 119, 122, 143

artists, use of blockchain technology by, 176–178

Ascendas-Singbridge, 162

Asia, smart cities of, 159–163

ASIC (application-specific integrated circuit), 93

audit trails, 134

Augur, 177

Australia, digital currencies, 132

Azure
Active Directory (AD), 116, 118
Azure Quickstart Templates, 113, 114
Azure Resource Manager, 113, 114
Azure Stack program, 113
BlockApps, 117
building in, 113–114
Chain, 114–116
Cortana, 116, 117
deploying blockchain tools on, 116–117
as digital ecosystem and cloud computing platform, 113
Ether.Camp, 117
Power BI, 116, 117–118

B

back up, 187–189

Badbitcoin.org, 47

Baltin, Alex (UBS Innovation Manager), 148

Bank for International Settlements, 133

Bank of America, 165

Bank of Singapore, 165

The Bank of Tokyo-Mitsubish UFJ Ltd, 165

banking trends, 131–135

Barclays, 137, 164

E

Notes

Notes

About the Author

Tiana Laurence is a co-founder of Factom, Inc., and was an early Bitcoin enthusiast. Her passion is growing great companies. A serial entrepreneur, Tiana started her first business at 16. She loves helping young aspiring entrepreneurs learn about business and technology. Tiana has a BA in Business and Leadership from Portland State University. When Tiana is not working on her businesses or being nerdy, she can be found running or rock climbing in Austin, Texas.

Dedication

This one is for Crystal and Jessica, for all the support and encouragement they gave me as I was writing this book.

Author's Acknowledgments

This book is the product of many people's ideas and work. It would not have been possible without the open and supportive blockchain and cryptocurrency world. I'd like to thank specifically Paul Snow, Peter Kirby, Brian Deery, and David Johnston for the countless hours spent teaching me about blockchain and cryptography. I'd also like to thank Abhi Dobhal, Lawrence Rufrano, Ryan Fugger, Charley Cooper, Alyse Killeen, Jeremy Kandah, Clemens Wan, Greg Wallace, Brian Behlendorf, Amir Chetrit, Jared Tate, Casey Lawlor, and Scott Robinson for the direction and guidance in the evolving blockchain space and for taking time out of their busy lives to review and sanity-check my work.

This book also took a lot of editing. I'm not kidding it really took a lot of editing. My project editor, Elizabeth Kuball, did a great job keeping me on task and on schedule, and Steve Hayes, my executive editor, made the whole book possible. I'd also like to thank Scott Robinson again for his thorough technical review and excellent suggestions, as well as editor Pat O'Brien and all the other behind-the-scenes people, who did thankless jobs to bring this book about. I'm forever in their debit.

Publisher's Acknowledgments

Executive Editor: Steve Hayes
Project Editor: Elizabeth Kuball
Copy Editor: Elizabeth Kuball
Technical Editor: Scott Robinson
Editorial Assistant: Serena Novosel
Sr. Editorial Assistant: Cherie Case

Production Editor: Magesh Elangovan
Cover Image: © the-lightwriter/iStockphoto

Apple & Mac

iPad For Dummies,
6th Edition
978-1-118-72306-7

iPhone For Dummies,
7th Edition
978-1-118-69083-3

Macs All-in-One
For Dummies, 4th Edition
978-1-118-82210-4

OS X Mavericks
For Dummies
978-1-118-69188-5

Blogging & Social Media

Facebook For Dummies,
5th Edition
978-1-118-63312-0

Social Media Engagement
For Dummies
978-1-118-53019-1

WordPress For Dummies,
6th Edition
978-1-118-79161-5

Business

Stock Investing
For Dummies, 4th Edition
978-1-118-37678-2

Investing For Dummies,
6th Edition
978-0-470-90545-6

Personal Finance
For Dummies, 7th Edition
978-1-118-11785-9

QuickBooks 2014
For Dummies
978-1-118-72005-9

Small Business Marketing
Kit For Dummies,
3rd Edition
978-1-118-31183-7

Careers

Job Interviews
For Dummies, 4th Edition
978-1-118-11290-8

Job Searching with Social
Media For Dummies,
2nd Edition
978-1-118-67856-5

Personal Branding
For Dummies
978-1-118-11792-7

Resumes For Dummies,
6th Edition
978-0-470-87361-8

Starting an Etsy Business
For Dummies, 2nd Edition
978-1-118-59024-9

Diet & Nutrition

Belly Fat Diet For Dummies
978-1-118-34585-6

Mediterranean Diet
For Dummies
978-1-118-71525-3

Nutrition For Dummies,
5th Edition
978-0-470-93231-5

Digital Photography

Digital SLR Photography
All-in-One For Dummies,
2nd Edition
978-1-118-59082-9

Digital SLR Video &
Filmmaking For Dummies
978-1-118-36598-4

Photoshop Elements 12
For Dummies
978-1-118-72714-0

Gardening

Herb Gardening
For Dummies, 2nd Edition
978-0-470-61778-6

Gardening with Free-Range
Chickens For Dummies
978-1-118-54754-0

Health

Boosting Your Immunity
For Dummies
978-1-118-40200-9

Diabetes For Dummies,
4th Edition
978-1-118-29447-5

Living Paleo For Dummies
978-1-118-29405-5

Big Data

Big Data For Dummies
978-1-118-50422-2

Data Visualization
For Dummies
978-1-118-50289-1

Hadoop For Dummies
978-1-118-60755-8

Language &
Foreign Language

500 Spanish Verbs
For Dummies
978-1-118-02382-2

English Grammar
For Dummies, 2nd Edition
978-0-470-54664-2

French All-in-One
For Dummies
978-1-118-22815-9

German Essentials
For Dummies
978-1-118-18422-6

Italian For Dummies,
2nd Edition
978-1-118-00465-4

Available in print and e-book formats.

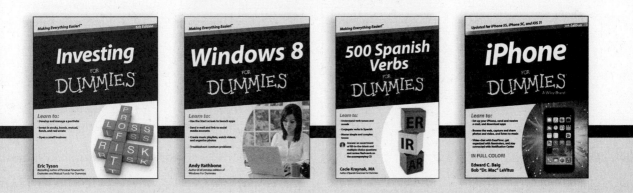

Available wherever books are sold. **For more information or to order direct visit www.dummies.com**

Math & Science

Algebra I For Dummies,
2nd Edition
978-0-470-55964-2

Anatomy and Physiology
For Dummies, 2nd Edition
978-0-470-92326-9

Astronomy For Dummies,
3rd Edition
978-1-118-37697-3

Biology For Dummies,
2nd Edition
978-0-470-59875-7

Chemistry For Dummies,
2nd Edition
978-1-118-00730-3

1001 Algebra II Practice
Problems For Dummies
978-1-118-44662-1

Microsoft Office

Excel 2013 For Dummies
978-1-118-51012-4

Office 2013 All-in-One
For Dummies
978-1-118-51636-2

PowerPoint 2013
For Dummies
978-1-118-50253-2

Word 2013 For Dummies
978-1-118-49123-2

Music

Blues Harmonica
For Dummies
978-1-118-25269-7

Guitar For Dummies,
3rd Edition
978-1-118-11554-1

iPod & iTunes
For Dummies, 10th Edition
978-1-118-50864-0

Programming

Beginning Programming
with C For Dummies
978-1-118-73763-7

Excel VBA Programming
For Dummies, 3rd Edition
978-1-118-49037-2

Java For Dummies,
6th Edition
978-1-118-40780-6

Religion & Inspiration

The Bible For Dummies
978-0-7645-5296-0

Buddhism For Dummies,
2nd Edition
978-1-118-02379-2

Catholicism For Dummies,
2nd Edition
978-1-118-07778-8

Self-Help &
Relationships

Beating Sugar Addiction
For Dummies
978-1-118-54645-1

Meditation For Dummies,
3rd Edition
978-1-118-29144-3

Seniors

Laptops For Seniors
For Dummies, 3rd Edition
978-1-118-71105-7

Computers For Seniors
For Dummies, 3rd Edition
978-1-118-11553-4

iPad For Seniors
For Dummies, 6th Edition
978-1-118-72826-0

Social Security
For Dummies
978-1-118-20573-0

Smartphones & Tablets

Android Phones
For Dummies, 2nd Edition
978-1-118-72030-1

Nexus Tablets
For Dummies
978-1-118-77243-0

Samsung Galaxy S 4
For Dummies
978-1-118-64222-1

Samsung Galaxy Tabs
For Dummies
978-1-118-77294-2

Test Prep

ACT For Dummies,
5th Edition
978-1-118-01259-8

ASVAB For Dummies,
3rd Edition
978-0-470-63760-9

GRE For Dummies,
7th Edition
978-0-470-88921-3

Officer Candidate Tests
For Dummies
978-0-470-59876-4

Physician's Assistant Exam
For Dummies
978-1-118-11556-5

Series 7 Exam For Dummies
978-0-470-09932-2

Windows 8

Windows 8.1 All-in-One
For Dummies
978-1-118-82087-2

Windows 8.1 For Dummies
978-1-118-82121-3

Windows 8.1 For Dummies,
Book + DVD Bundle
978-1-118-82107-7

e **Available in print and e-book formats.**

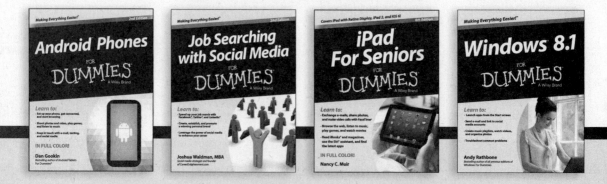

Available wherever books are sold. **For more information or to order direct visit www.dummies.com**

Take Dummies with you everywhere you go!

Whether you are excited about e-books, want more from the web, must have your mobile apps, or are swept up in social media, Dummies makes everything easier.

Leverage the Power

For Dummies is the global leader in the reference category and one of the most trusted and highly regarded brands in the world. No longer just focused on books, customers now have access to the For Dummies content they need in the format they want. Let us help you develop a solution that will fit your brand and help you connect with your customers.

Advertising & Sponsorships

Connect with an engaged audience on a powerful multimedia site, and position your message alongside expert how-to content.

Targeted ads • Video • Email marketing • Microsites • Sweepstakes sponsorship

Dummies products make life easier!

- DIY
- Consumer Electronics
- Crafts
- Software
- Cookware
- Hobbies
- Videos
- Music
- Games
- and More!

For more information, go to **Dummies.com** and search the store by category.

FOR
DUMMIES
A Wiley Brand